Shooting Cinematic Videos on the

iPhone SE 2020

CAMERA

A Step by Step Approach to Taking Professional Photographs and Shooting Cinematic Videos on the 2020 iPhone SE

DONALD RAY

Copyright

Donald Ray
ISBN: 9798650116912
ChurchGate Publishing House
USA | UK | Canada
© Churchgate Publishing House 2020

Table of Contents

Chapter 3

SHOOTING CINEMATIC VIDEOS

Chapter 4

HOW TO CONFIGURE FILMING SPEED ON THE iPhone SE 2020

Chapter 5

Using FilMic Pro App for Cinematic Shots on the iPhone SE 2020

Chapter 1

INTRODUCTION TO IPHONE SE 2020 PHOTOGRAPHY

Recently, Apple declared a second-generation iPhone SE, a sophisticated novel iPhone featuring an assemblage of new functions. From a 4.7-inch Retina HD display coupled with Touch ID, which caters to industry-leading security. IPhone SE comes in a compact design, re-overhauled from inside out, and is the most economical iPhone. The novel iPhone SE is packaged with the Apple-designed A13 Bionic, which can handle the most complicated of tasks. IPhone SE also has one of the best single-camera systems in an iPhone.

The single-camera can unknot the advantages of computational photography, which includes portrait mode and ability to withstand elements with specks of dust and water. With the novel iPhone SE, three beautiful colors exist— black, white, and red. According to Phil Schiller, Apple's senior vice president of Worldwide Marketing, "iPhone SE incorporates the industry-leading performance of A13 bionic that ensures great battery life, shoots stunning portrait mode and smart HDR photos. It also has the power to shoot amazing videos with stereo audio". Without much ado, the following are new functions in iPhone SE 2020;

Popular Design with 4.7-inch Display

The iPhone SE 2020 has as one of its features, a graded aluminum, and a durable glass design plus front, which is available in black, red, and white. A centered Apple logo, which features in the rear glass finish, is made by using a seven-layer color technique for accurate hue and opacity and giving a color-matched aluminum band. It resists dust and water up to 1meter for 30minutes. The Retina HD display with 4.7-inch has a pure tone that adjusts the white balance to equate the ambient light for a more natural, paper-like viewing experience.

The sparkling broad color HD Retina display exudes incredible color perfection. It also supports Dolby Vision and HDR 10 playback. IPhone SE has Hepatic Touch for fast actions. Actions such as animating live photos, message previewing, and applications rearranging. IPhone SE also incorporates the familiar home button designed with Sapphire crystal to give protection to the sensor and make it more durable. There is a presence of a steel ring to detect a user's fingerprint for Touch ID. A smooth, private, and secure alternative to entering a password to unlock iPhone are by using the Touch ID.

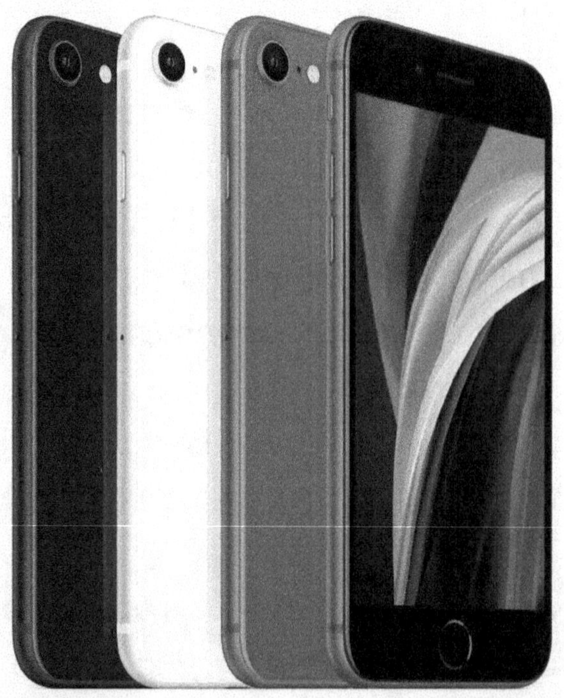

The three beautiful colors of the iPhone SE 2020. Black, white, and red designed to resist water and dust.

The smartest chip in a Smartphone— A13 Bionic

The first categories of iPhone type that the A13 Bionic was introduced to were iPhone 11 and iPhone 11 pro. The A13 Bionic is the quickest ever in a Smartphone with a unique performance for every task iPhone SE performs. The iPhone SE 2020 is a good fit for photography and augmented reality. A13 Bionic enables every action to feel fluid. The A13 Bionic was developed with consideration on machine learning. It has an 8-Core Neural Engine capable of executing 5 trillion operations per second, a dual machine learning accelerator, and a new machine learning controller to equilibrate performance and efficiency.

Both A13 Bionic and iOS 13 allow new brilliant applications that use Core ML and machine learning. The A13 Bionic also improves battery life for iPhone SE. The wireless-charging iPhone SE with Qi-certified chargers allows quick-charging relaying to customers up to 50% charge in 30 minutes. Also available is lighting-fast download speed incorporated with Wi-Fi 6 and Gigabit-class LTE. The presence of dual SIM plus eSIM allows for flexibility for users to have two different phone numbers on a single device while traveling abroad.

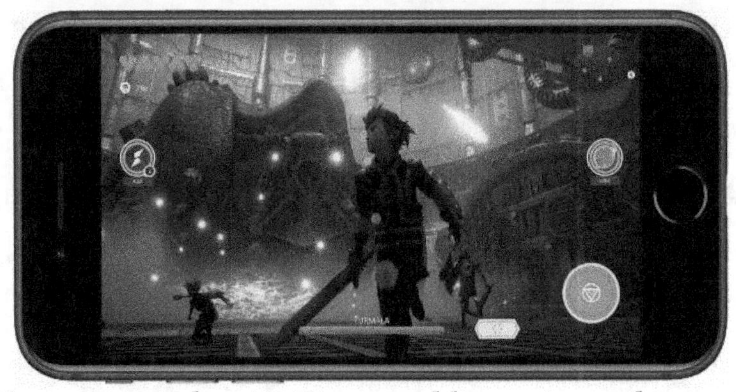

iPhone SE 2020 has A13 Bionic enabling to Strong battery life and efficiency

Introduction to iPhone SE 2020 Camera

The same 12MB single-camera present in iPhone 8 also features in Apple's iPhone SE. It adopts a Sony sensor with a 1.2 micrometer pitch behind 28mm f/1.8lens. The availability of optical stabilization and detection autofocus also exists. The lenses of the camera are factory-calibrated to give superior performance in AR. Also available on the iPhone SE is the quad-LED dual-tone flash. The quad-LED supports flash, which is slow-sync. It keeps the shutter ajar for a bit longer permitted in some of the ambient light, which in turn produces natural images. Due to the incorporation of A13 Bionic chip and its ISP, the camera now supports portrait mode based singly on a depth map curated by a machine learning process, as seen with a selfie camera. The most recent Apple smart HDR from iPhone 11 generation also exists on the iphone SE with a significant increase in image quality. It is essential to state here that the new Night Mode, which exists in the iphone 11 series, is missing in the SE. Like the front-face camera, we saw on iphone 7 and 8, iphone SE also has a front-face camera of 7MP. There is a Retina flash where the screen illuminates your face in an array of colors, which results in increased skin tones with respect to the available light color.

Camera app

There have been incremental changes over the years on the camera app. It has the same interface with a swipe-able mode that has existed for quite a while now. All images and video settings aren't featured in the camera app. To resolve this, the camera must be closed, go to settings, and return to the camera. The human subject is the only section where the portrait mode works. It isn't that the camera is unable to construct a depth map but because Apple opposed it.

With the iPhone SE, natural-looking pictures can be taken. The absence of noise; top-notch colors, and a varying range and contrast make it a must have. The details are very good, jaw-dropping at some spots though there are many challenges that turn out for the camera. There has been an improvement in the low-light performance since iPhone 8 by a wider if the same camera takes the images. Due to reduced noise, they have sufficient resolved details. The saturation of the color is excellent with real-life colors. The dynamic range isn't the best, but a single camera can do much. Although Apple didn't bring forth the Night Mode on the iPhone SE, a portrait mode was infused. In line with the portrait, the shots taken from the rear camera were okay.

Selfie

The quality of pictures taken from 7MP iPhone SE outweighs that taken from 20MP and 32MP Quad-Bayer shooters on a range of Android phones. The image of iPhone SE 7MP exudes exceptional detail, dynamic range, and contrast. The iPhone SE shooter also can perform portraits and can achieve that with utmost proficiency. The subject separation and bokeh simulation are remarkable.

Video Recording

Apple iphone SE captures videos in all popular resolution frames and is optically stabilized. The 30fps videos also include video stabilization and broad dynamic range due to Smart HDR. It's important to state that iPhone SE can do 1080P at 240fps. Also, the video bitrate is around 45Mbps in 4K and 30fps, 100Mbps for 4K at 60fps. The 4K videos are shot at 30fbs. The colors and contrast are excellent, with absence of compression artifacts. The 1080p videos, 30fps or 60fps are detail-oriented, superb foliage, and impressive variable range. The cinematic and the optical stabilization work in all frame resolutions, both on the main and selfie camera.

Physical features of the iPhone SE 2020 camera

Rear camera

In a bid to be economical, a single-lens rear camera is featured on the iPhone SE but never adopts any technology from iPhone 11 and 11pro. In essence, this means that better photos were possible with the iphone 8. The iPhone SE is using the same 12-megapixel rear camera sensor as iphone 8. What makes the former unique is that it benefits from the A13's improved image signal processor. The 12-megapixel broad-angle camera incorporates an f/1.8 aperture together with optical image stabilization and a variety of color captures the most recent generation Smart HRD for advanced highlight and details of shadow. According to the iPhone, it's the best single-camera ever existed.

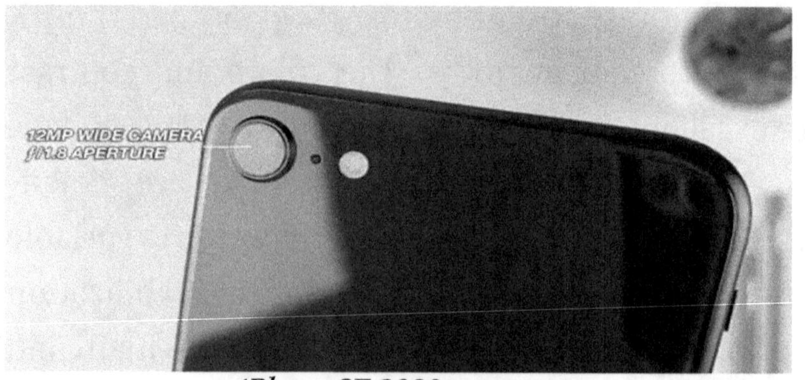

iPhone SE 2020 rear camera

Front camera

The 7MP front-facing camera has an f/2.2 aperture with depth control support and portrait mode despite the absence of a TrueDepth camera system. The features are activated by the use of machine learning and monocular depth evaluation. The front-face camera enables quick take. It's interesting to note that iphone SE is the class of iPhones that offers this feature. The recording of 1080p HD video can be done at 30 frames per second. It has other functions, including Retina flash, auto image stabilization, burst mode, and full-color capture.

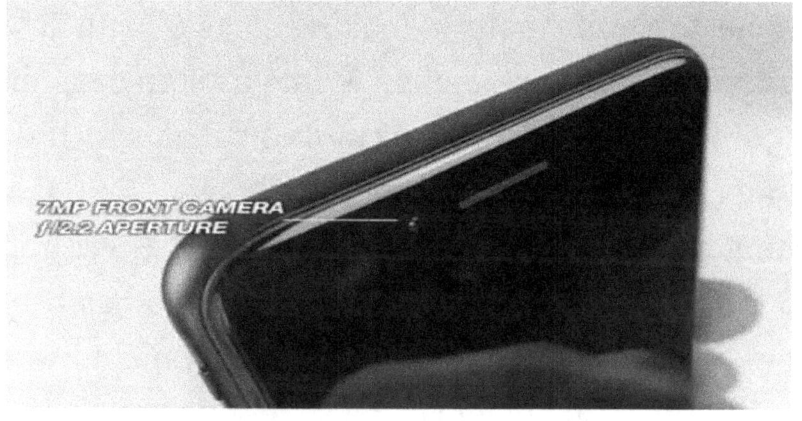

iPhone SE 2020 front camera

Basic functions of iPhone SE 2020 Camera

One of the peculiar features offered by iPhone SE is a juicy single-camera that's known in an iPhone with 12-megapixel and employs the image signal processor and neural engine of A13 Bionic to unknot the more advantages of computational photography, portrait mode, and six portrait lighting effect.

With the exploration of machine learning and monocular depth estimation, iPhone SE can take fantastic portrait photos with the front camera. Smart HDR of next-generation features in iPhone SE. Intelligent re-lighting can identify subjects in a frame for more natural-looking images with jaw-dropping shadow-details. With a stereo audio recording and film stabilization on rear and front cameras, videos are more immersive. The rear camera allows for videos high-quality of 4k with up to 60fps, and a stretched dynamic range has been seen in iPhone SE for more detail highlights with up to 30fps. Customers can also leverage on Quick-take video on front and rear cameras.

How to take photography in burst mode
Burst mode has the ability to take a large number of high-speed photos so to give you an array of photos to choose from. Burst photos can be taken with the front and rear cameras. Follow the steps below in taking a burst photo on your iPhone SE 2020;

• Kindly swipe the shutter button to the left, to take recurring-fire pictures.

• Remove your finger to stop

• Select a photo of your choice by tapping the Burst thumbnail.

- Click the circle on the lower-right angle of every photo you intend saving as a unit photo
- Tap Done
- Click on the thumbnail to delete the whole burst

Night mode photograph

The iPhone SE 2020 doesn't support this function.

How to apply a filter to photos on iPhone SE 2020

- Do to photo then tap a photo or video thumbnail to have a look on the full screen.
- Click on edit, followed by tapping on three dots to apply the filter effect. The filter effect ranges from vivid, Silverstone, and dramatic.
- Click on a filter and move the slider to adjust the effect
- Click on photo to compare the original picture from the edited.
- To save your edits, tap Done.
- Tap cancel if you do not like your changes followed by clicking discard changes.

How to set up self-timer for camera

It's easy to put yourself in the picture using the self-timer on your native camera application's iPhone. To achieve this, follow these steps;

- Open the camera application on your iPhone.

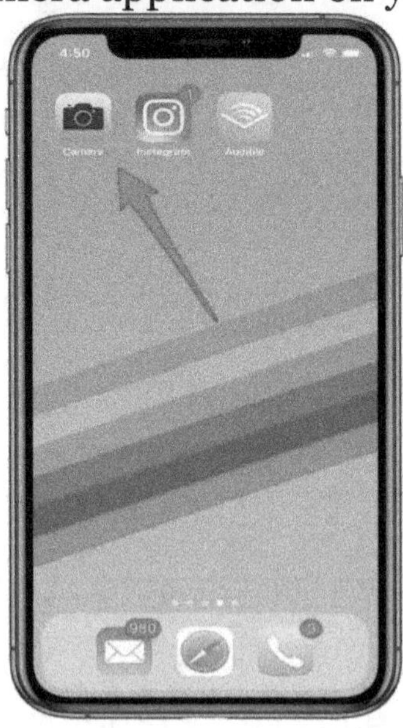

- Set up the shot you wish to take and ensure you leave room for yourself.

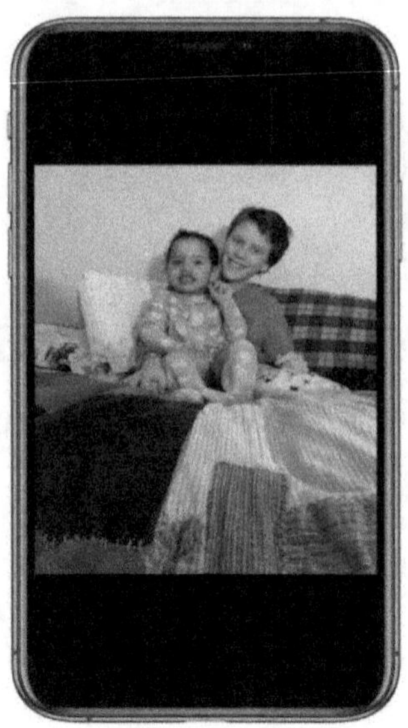

- Click on the timer icon. Here, you can choose between a 3-second timer and a 10-second one.

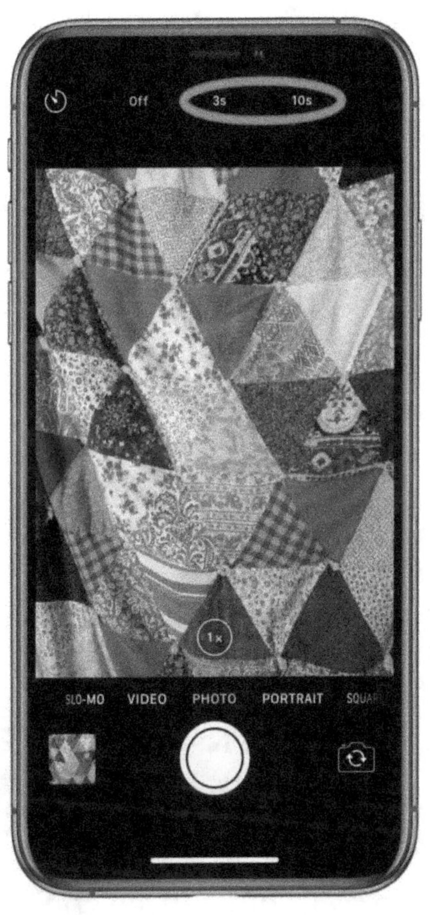

- In case you didn't see a timer icon at the top of your screen, click the arrow in the top corner of your screen, and the timer icon will show just above the shutter button.

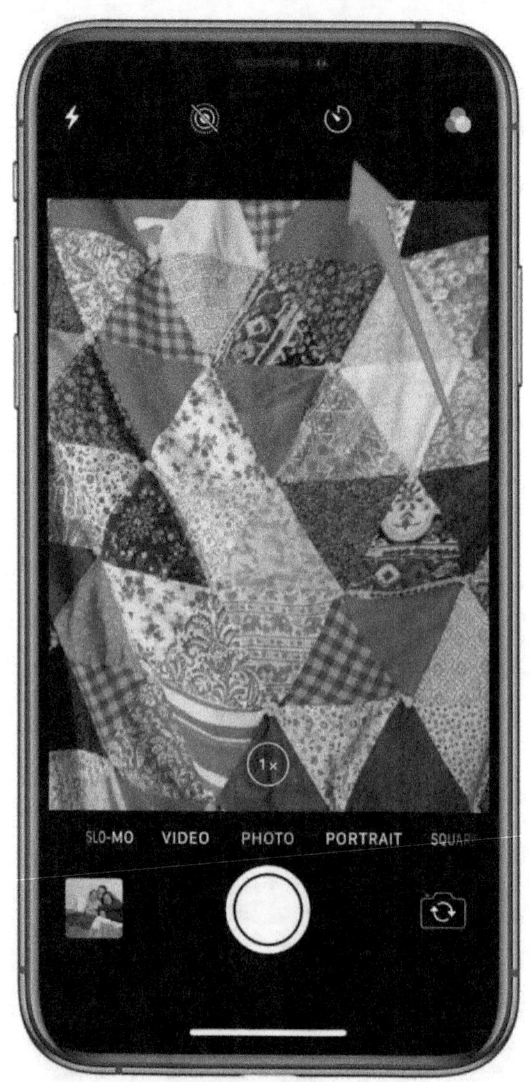

- Select the countdown time you prefer.

- Click the shutter release and wait for the connection to finish.

- You have time to get yourself stabilized in the picture.

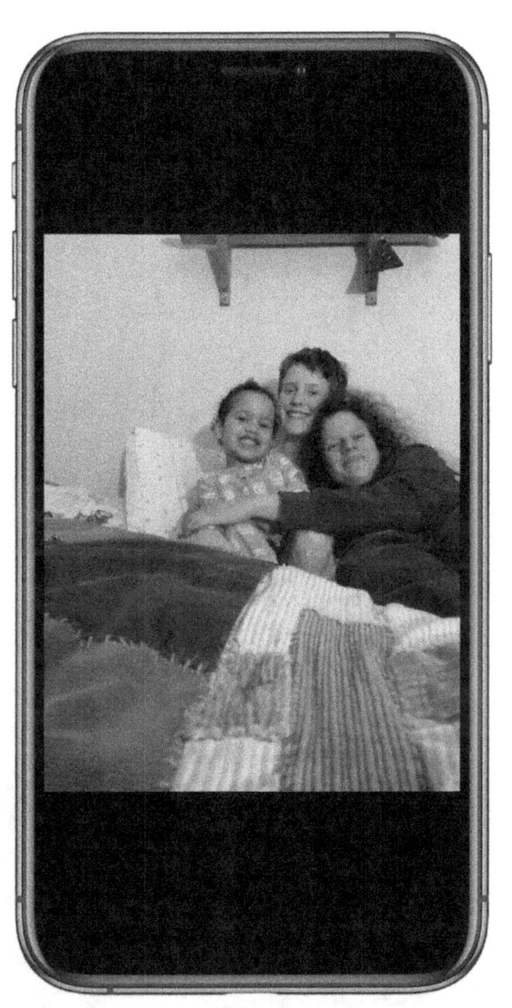

How to take a live photo

- Open the camera app.
- Ensure your camera is set to photo mode. Make sure you turn on live photo.
- Hold your device.
- Click on the shutter button.

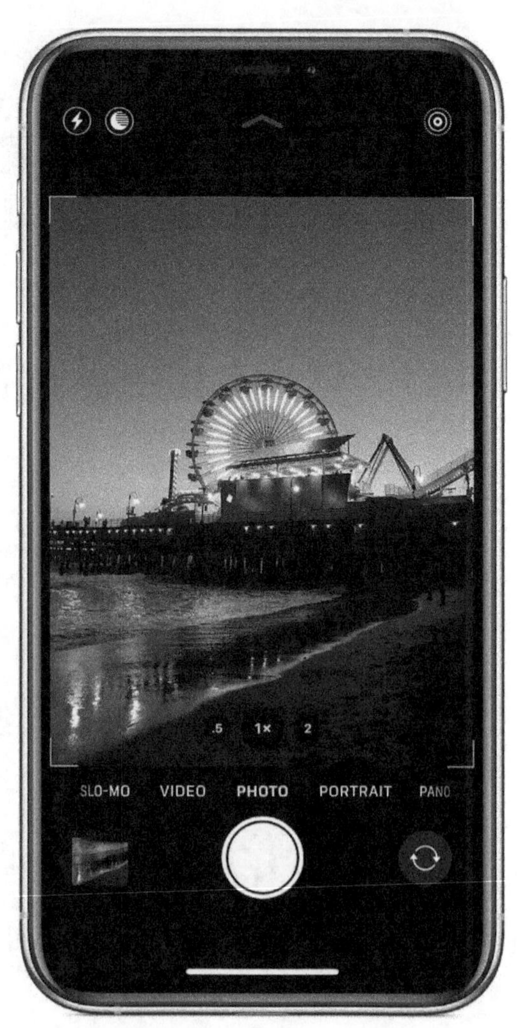

How to take selfie

With the front camera in the photo mode, you can take a selfie with your iphone SE 2020. The following are steps to achieve that;

• Click on the camera frame to switch to the front camera.

• Hold your iPhone SE in front of you.

• Click on the shutter button and press either volume button to action the shot.

Chapter 2

CAMERA MODES ON iPHONE SE 2020

Portrait mode

Portrait mode employs the cameras in iPhone models to curate a depth-of-field-effect. With this, you can take a picture that allows your subject to be sharp while providing a blur to the background. To your photo, you also can add lighting effects and take a selfie in portrait mode.

How to take pictures in portrait mode
• Open the camera app and swipe to portrait mode

• Follow the hints on your screen. When the portrait mode is ready, the lighting effect's name will change. For natural light, it turns yellow.

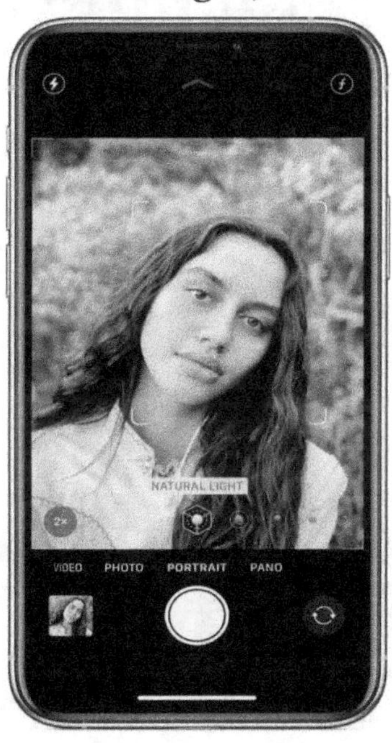

-   Click the shutter button

• the camera allows you to know when you are too far, too close and in dark zones. After you might have taken the photos, you can deploy the built-in editing features to crop.

Portrait lighting

• Open the photo app and select a portrait mode photo you intend to change
• Click edit to ensure that lighting effect appear below the photo

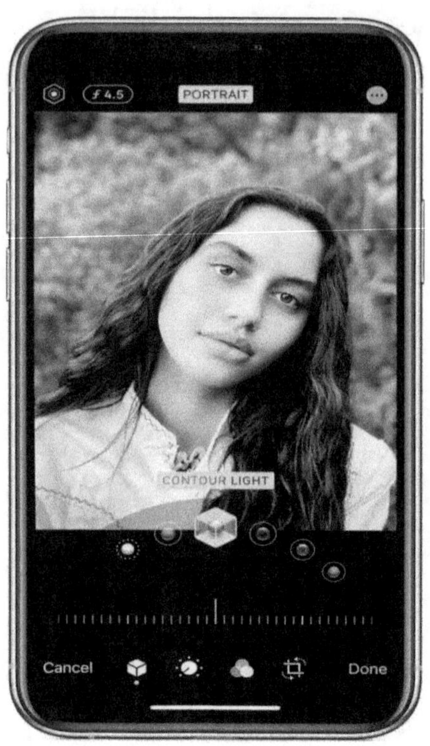

• Swipe on the lighting effect to select from the one you want.

• Click on done to finish.

How to take a selfie in portrait mode

• Open the camera app

• Swipe to portrait mode and click on the front camera button

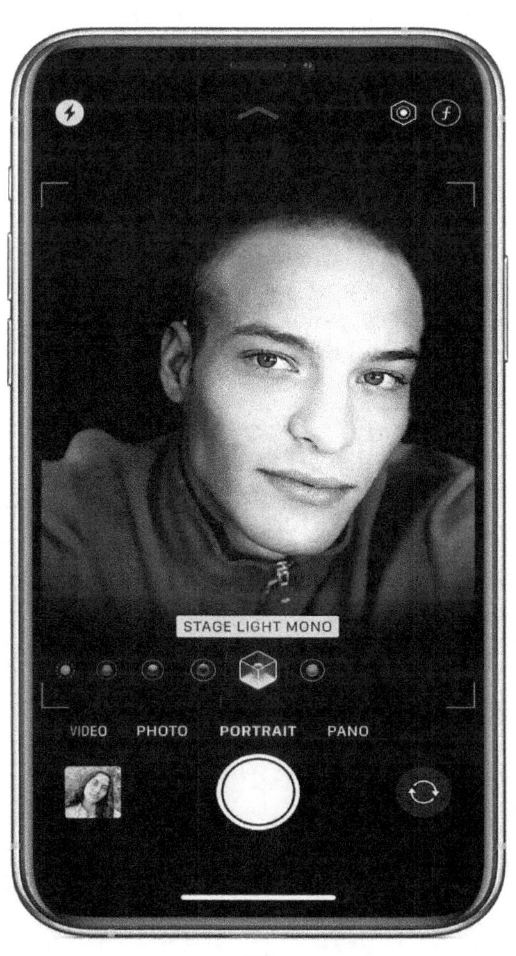

- Hold your iphone close to your face
- Snap you selfie with one of the volume buttons.

Depth control adjustment and portrait lighting

- Click a portrait mode photo in your gallery.
- Click edit and tap the depth control button at the top of the screen to adjust the portrait lighting to adjust portrait lighting.
- A slider would pops up, move it right or left to adjust the effect.
- Click on Done.

How to Remove Portrait Mode Effect

- Choose the picture that you intend changing
- Click Edit
- Tap portrait at the top of your screen

PANO Mode

Ever thought of capturing a breakthrough land-scape but the view on your camera screen won't accommodate such? A pano mode is here to resolve the dilemma. Pano mode provides you with a guide bar in the middle of the screen to assist you take your picture. If you wish to initiate the photo from the left, ensure the arrow is directing to the right. If you are starting from the right, click the arrow and change its direction. Click the shutter button and gently move your camera in a starting line from one side of your shot to the next. Also, ensure you keep the arrow on the guide bar.

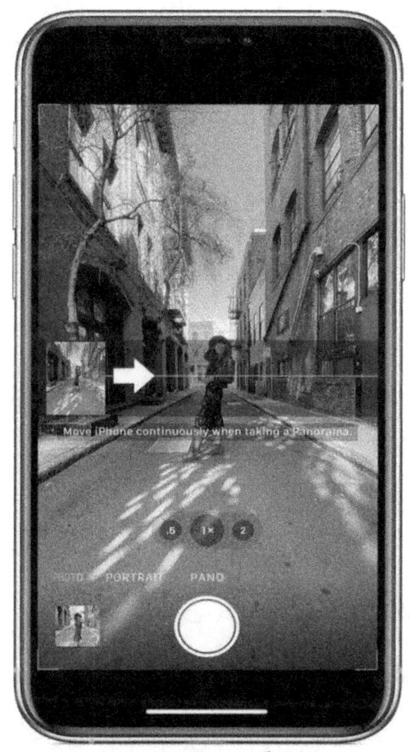

Pano mode

SQUARE Mode

Square mode configures the frame of your camera screen to a square. The square mode is the optimal size for several social media applications. When you take a picture, you can share it on your most preferred media platform.

SLO-MO

The slow-motion video has been in existence for a while now. Slow-motion allows you to shoot at a high frame per second. After you have finished recording, go back to slow or accelerate a specific part of the video. This is pretty much interesting to shoot when you engage in hyper-fast action shots. To operate in Slow mode;

• Launch the camera app on your iPhone

• Ensure you swipe right in twofold, given that you are on the photo mode by default. You can also click the word Slo-Mo in the bottom left.

• Click on the **Record** button to initiate the recording of your slow motion video

• Click on the **Stop** button to end the recording.

TIME-LAPSE Mode

This captures footage at selected intervals to create a time-lapse video that's fast and easy to share. When you go to time-lapse mode, click on the shutter button. Your camera takes pictures at intervals until you click on the shutter button again.

Chapter 3

SHOOTING CINEMATIC VIDEOS

The era of black and white TV is long gone the moment the colored television became more widespread in the USA. But in this century, we can still some cinematographers shooting videos that look more like it was shot in the '60s. This is not supposed to be so as the advent of colored TV has even made things especially very easy, now, than ever before.

Most times, people see a photograph and start doubting if it was a photograph or a live painting. Most live arts have a high color transition, which makes them appear real pictures. If you want your videos to look as if the actors are performing live – just like in the cinema – then you have to give them some finishing topnotch finishing touches. A cinematic video is a video that looks like a film. The color animation, lighting frequency, aspect ratios, and many other features should be of high quality if you want to have a cinematic video. Nowadays, merely buying the right camera is no longer enough to have that cinematic effect you'd like to give your video. There are now systematic approaches in place that can guarantee you the best quality shot you can only dream of, even if you are using a mid-range camera.

Here are some few tips to give you the much desired cinematic effect in your video;

24fps over 30fps: The movies you see at the cinema were all shot at a 24 frame rate. Contrary to the belief people have that higher frame rates connote more top quality, 24fps is the real deal if you want to have that cinematic appearance. Just because a camera can shoot at a very high frame rate per second doesn't mean you should watch the movie at that rate. Some cameras come with the default 30fps, but you can change it by yourself if you want.

Shallow depth of field over full depth of field: Most camcorders have a wide field, which doesn't give the desired cinematic effect. You might want to consider a DSLR type camera to provide you with an out-of-focus background. A shallow field of depth is preferable over a wide field of depth if a cinematic video is what you want.

Dolly camera movement over zooming: Dollying is a type of camera movement where the videographer moves the whole camera towards the subject/object, using track or motorized vehicle. Zooming doesn't necessarily provide the much desired cinematographic effect.

Don't compress the Video Image: To avoid compressing the video image, you should try and shoot in the RAW file format. This way, you will be transferring the exact pixel size onto your computer for easy editing on the editing software.

Excellent lighting: You don't have to be a professional before you set up cinematic lighting. With just a few lights arranged at the appropriate place, you should be able to make a cinematic video/image. The 5-in-1 reflector and some cheap LED lights will give you the best chance.

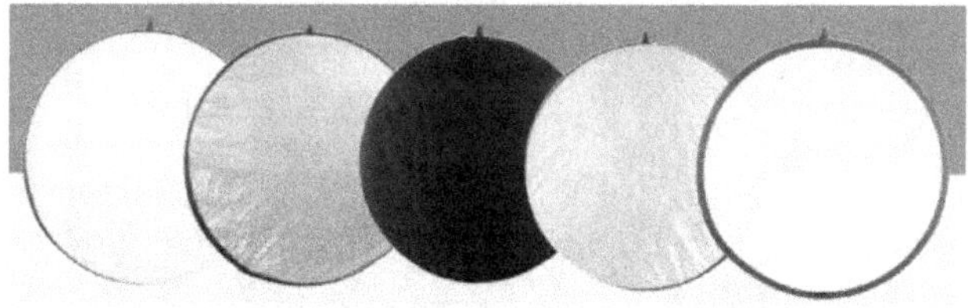

5-in-1 reflector

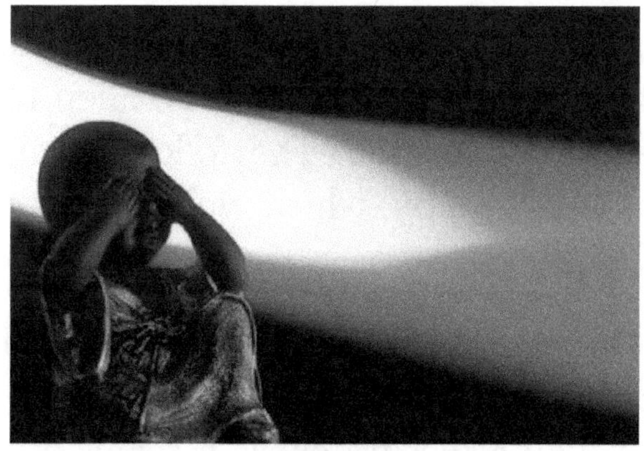

Led light effect

Use color grading where necessary: color grade all your footages before exporting them into the video editing software. This makes the video appear very cinematic. You can use the magic bullet from Red giant for this purpose. With the magic bullet, you can balance out your shots with high color adjustments.

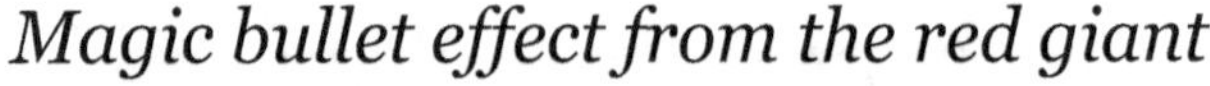

Magic bullet effect from the red giant

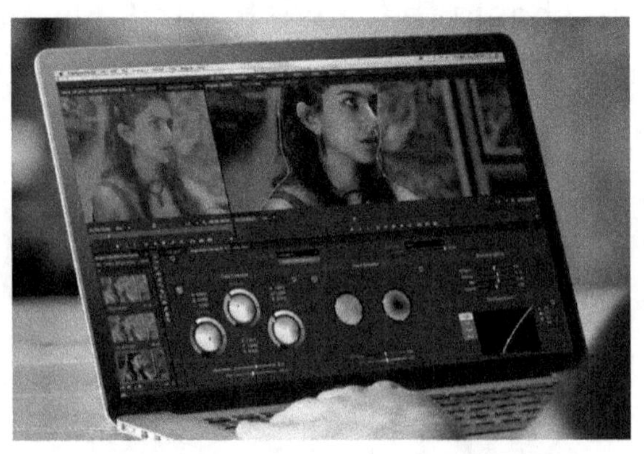

Video Terms Used in Cinematography

Every known profession have their terms deployed on the field. These terms might be alien to people who are not in the job. The following are terms used in videography which you can familiarize yourself with;

White Balance: This is the process of balancing your camera's color temperature so that we can represent light as accurately as it seems in real life.

Essentially, white balance is a camera function that informs the camera of the lighting condition you are filming with to remove the original color-cast from the image. Videographers often go through the process of editing image just to eliminate contrasting color cast, and make the picture matches what they see when they took the picture. Digital cameras don't have the exact technology yet to accurately guess what the color temperature of the surrounding of the image is, just like our brain can do. Digital cameras, especially phone cameras, often make errors while trying to guess the surrounding color temperature, and adjust themselves accordingly. Because of this error, some of the pictures taken might appear to be unnecessarily bluish or yellow, and the skin tone might look unreal.

Correct White Background and Incorrect White Background

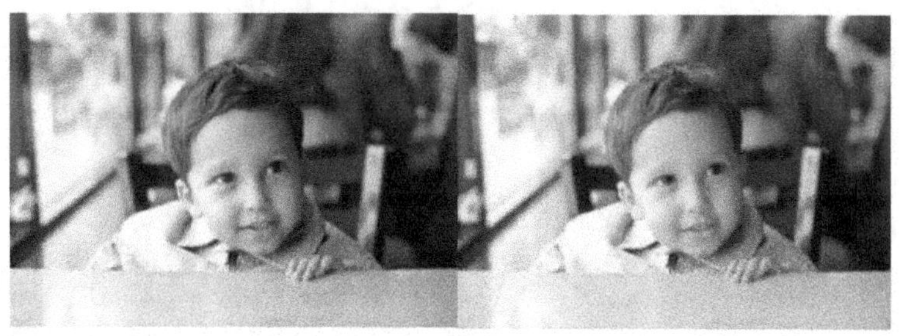

The second image above needs the white balance adjusted to remove the yellow tone.

Frame Rate Per Second (fps):   some people don't know that video is a series of standing image, that when viewed at a particular speed will make it seems as if the pictures were moving. Each image you see in a photograph represents a frame, and the speed with which those images are shown is called frame rate per second. A video captured at 24fps implies that 24 distinct images are shown each second of the video. The frame rate significantly impacts video appearance. Choosing a frame rate is deciding how natural you want your video to appear. Apple upgraded the 4k 30fps to 60fps, together with a cinematographic worthy 24fps in the iPhone SE 2020. Apple understands the fact that 24fps is actually best for cinematic video. Movies are normally displayed in 24fps. This is because this film rate looks like how we see the world we live in. So natural! Live broadcast or a gaming event will probably need a higher fps; this is because many things need to be covered at once. Shutter speed: This is the actual length of time that your camera is exposed to light. The shutter is what enables the light to reach the digital sensor of your camera. Essentially, if the light that enters is not adequate, you will have a blurred image. From observation, the more you hold on to your camera, the more your hands begin to shake. This makes your hands cause noticeable blurring in the shot.

Therefore, you need a camera stabilization that can hold your camera for you while you take your shot. You can create a blurred image just by varying the shutter speed of your camera. The shutter in the iPhone SE 2020 is incorporated into the sensor of the camera. The shutter in the iPhone camera is opened all the time so that it can receive enough light to process a better image. On your iPhone, you can adjust the volume of your shutter's sound by pressing the volume up/down. Holding on to the shutter button on your device will keep it taking continuous pictures.

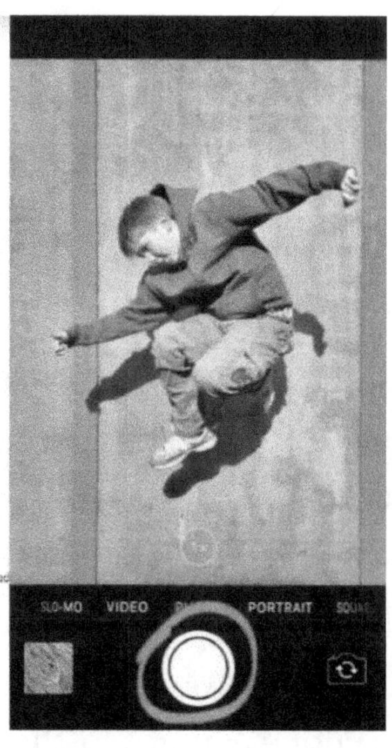

Shutter button highlighted in red in the above image

ISO: This feature measures the sensitivity of your device to light. It is rated in values, ranging from 100, 200, 400, 800 etc. The higher the number, the more your device's sensitivity to light. A higher number means you can use the camera in a low light situation, such as darkness.

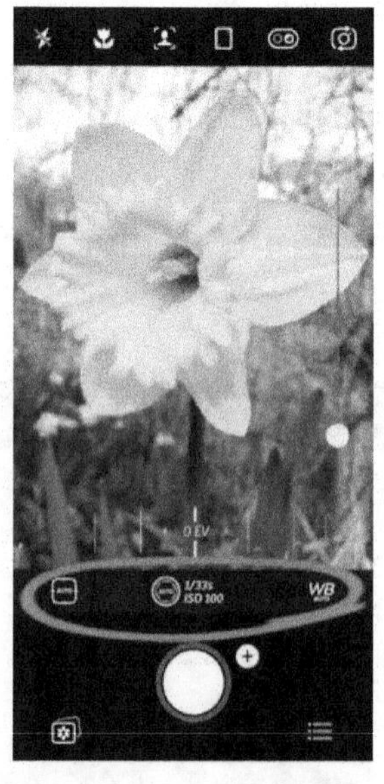

B-Roll: The B-roll gives you an idea of what is going on around a specific subject that you are shooting. Essentially, B-roll is any added footage that enhances the story so that your viewers become more engaged. B-roll is just like the secondary footage. A-roll is the central footage. Let us say you are using your iPhone camera to shoot an interview or a wedding – only when you redirect the camera from the person you are interviewing is called the B-roll. The A-roll is the interview you are making. Tips: for effective B-roll, try and get a smooth shot and a shallow depth of views. A shallow depth of view will throw the background out of focus if you concentrate on a single object or person in the B-roll.

Warp speed effect: This is used to take a motion picture, especially when you are in an underground situation. With your DLSR camera attached to your iPhone SE 2020, you can maximize this feature better. All you need to do is duct tape your iPhone to the back of the DSLR camera.

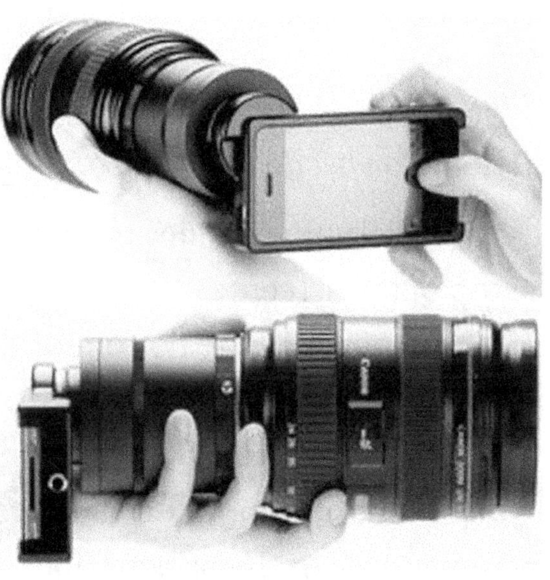

Phone mounted at the back of the DSLR camera

Control the Aperture and ISO of the DSLR so that the Shutter speed is between 1/10th of a second to 2 seconds. Lightly press the shutter to have your camera focus, then meter the light, and it will show you the shutter speed it is going to use. It is okay if the rate is within 1/10th to 2 seconds. If it is not, then change to a smaller ISO number, e.g., 100, or 200. Don't allow your camera to take a five or 10-second image; otherwise, it will just blur out everything.

Foreground: This is a cinematographic technique where the video captured things, objects, or people behind the subject – as long it doesn't distract the subject or the videographer.

How do you use the smart selection mode on your iPhone to specify the foreground?

From the smart selection mode, tap on the pencil icon at the top of the screen.

Tap on the focus menu at the bottom of the screen and simply draw a line inside the area you wish to keep in focus with your finger.

Navigate to the background icon and draw a line around the inner area of the background. The white line will indicate the area you want to focus on, and the black line is the area you wish to block. See the results below.

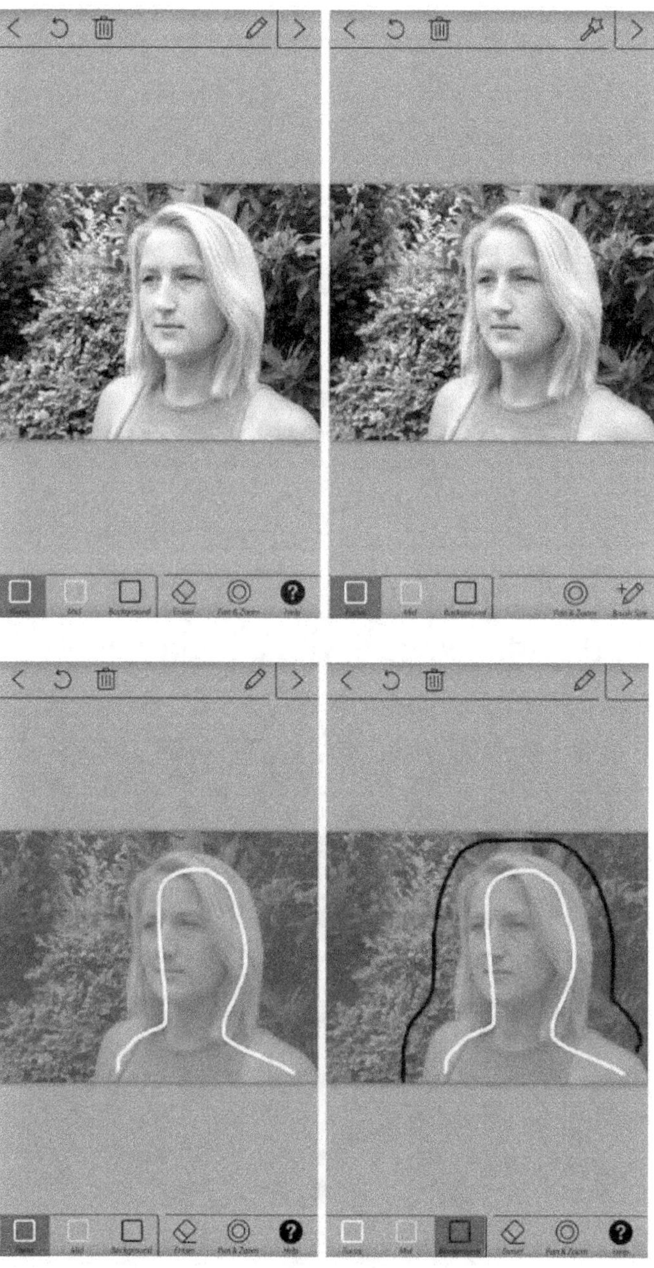

Depth of field: This is the distance of separation between the farthest and the closest object in your shootings. We can have a narrow depth of field and a tremendous depth of field. Have you ever tried to take a close-up shot of an object in front of you, but couldn't get the picture of the entire object in focus? If yes, then it is because you were too close to the object. The closer you are to an object in focus, the shallower the depth of view. Aperture also contributes to a good depth of field – the smaller the aperture, the better the depth of field. For better depth of field, the camera-object distance must be large. If you consider the pictures below, you will observe that the picture with a higher depth of field appears sharper.

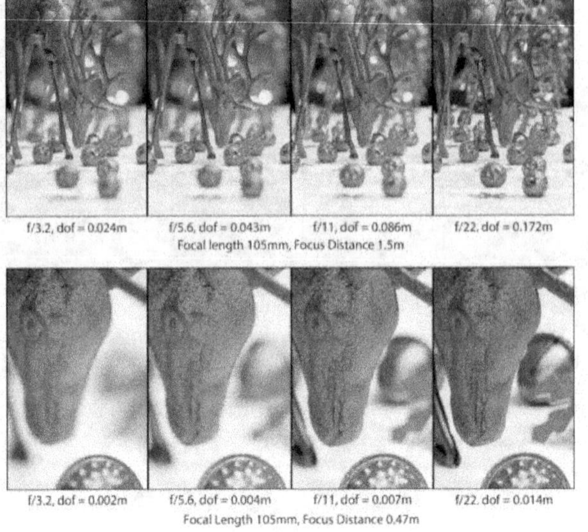

Note: To get a better idea of the depth of view, simply attach an external camera to your iphone SE 2020. A camera like Nikon D500 works better.

Accessories for Shooting Cinematic videos on

iPhone SE 2020

Expert and professional videographers typically use some costly and powerful cameras, such as camcorders, DSLR, ZV1 Digital Camera, etc., to achieve a powerful cinematographic effect. However, these cameras are too expensive for beginners, and it is advisable to make do with what we have. Iphones now come handy with sophisticated cameras that can produce mid-range, albeit robust videos to capture the viewer's attention. In fact, the latest technology can now enable the iphone record video in 4k format.

However, with many high-end iphone accessories, you can now turn your iphone into a professional cinematographic device. Find below some affordable iphone accessories that give a potent cinematographic effect;

Handheld Gimbal Stabilizer for iPhones: Many people find it especially difficult to shoot non-shaky videos with their smartphones. This is because they need to be moving around with their device. To prevent you from recording a video that will look blurry in quality, and file a smooth and consistent shot, you might consider attaching your iphone to a stabilizer. A gimbal stabilizer holds the iphone in shape to remove unwarranted shaky movement during recording. An easier-to-use and straightforward gimbal stabilizer you might want to consider is the Osmo mobile 3. If you want a gimbal you can take anywhere; I'd advise you to consider the Osmo mobile 3. It is portable and enables one-hand use coupled with user directive functions. Another less expensive gimbal device for iphone you might want to check out is the Feiyutech VLOG pocket. The VLOG pocket has a button where you can switch between portrait mode and landscape for your device.

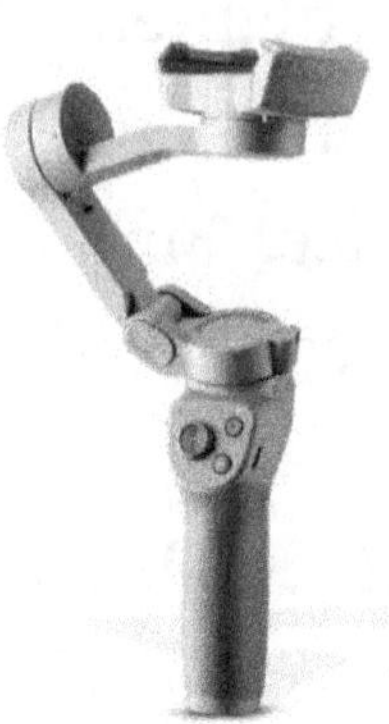

Osmo Mobile 3

- ○ **25X External telephoto zoom lens**: The dual type is preferable, as many users have given not-so-good reviews about the normal telephoto lens. The lens adjusts the distance between the eyepiece of the lens and the phone's camera, which makes the device perfect for shooting without any dark corner. It is particularly useful for shooting a very high-quality video.

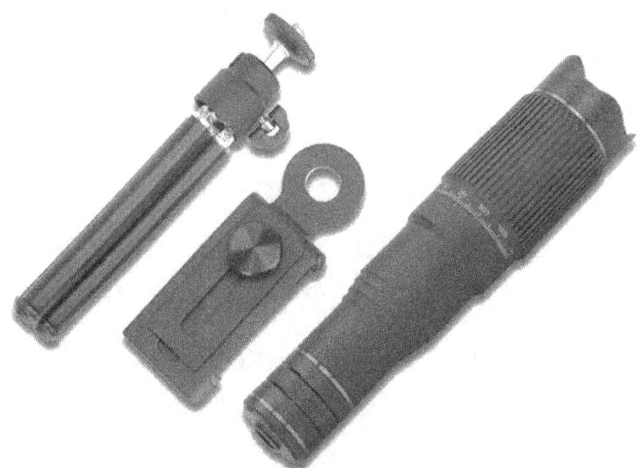

- ○ **Wide-angle 3-in-1 lens**: This will help you get maximum use from your device's camera. The wide-angle lens offers a sizeable magnification capable enough to zoom your object and have a direct focus on your camera. The fish eye design that comes with it enables you to give a unique fish eye effect to your videos and pictures.

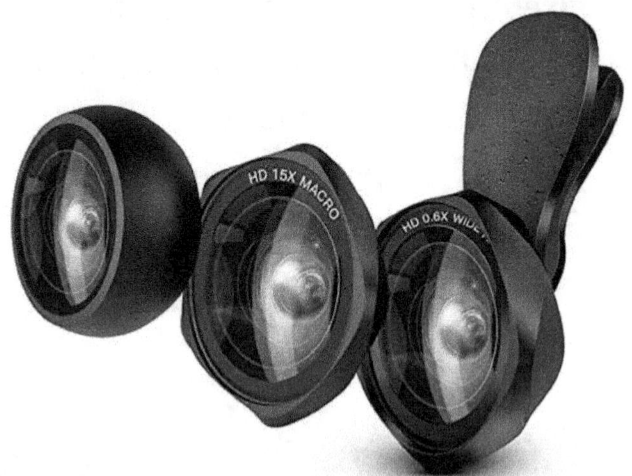

o **Rode Video Mic Me-L**: This microphone is an improvement to an inbuilt microphone that comes with iphone devices. When coupled with your iphone SE 2020, it provides an adorable sonic sound to your video recordings. The broader range of frequency in the device gives users a wide audible range. The microphone is designed to reject any sound hitting the sides of the microphone. Its directionality only enables it to receive sound from the object to which it is directly pointing toward.

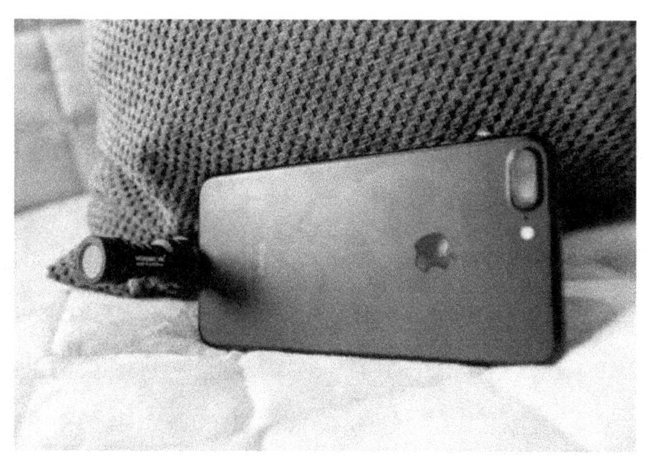

Rode Mic Me-L

o **SandMac Hybrid filter**: With this filter, landscape videography is now very perfect. The filter protects the camera from overexposure to light, thereby improving the high dynamic range of the phone camera. The lens provides your footage with a perfect cinematic appearance.

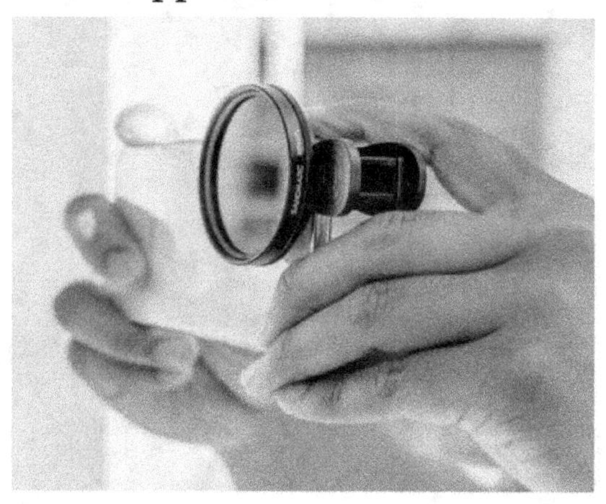

o **Adonit photogrip QI:** This is a multi-tool kit for those who love using their iPhone to record videos. The function lies in the grip itself, which expands to fit any device with just about any 4.5-inch or larger. The grip performs several functions. Its primary use is to give users a better grip on their iPhone, but it is much more useful than that. It is a wireless charger and has a 3000mAh battery capacity. If you cast it on your wireless-compatible iPhone, it'll charge the phone while you're busy recording videos and taking photos. The grip is chargeable with a USB-A or a USB-C type.

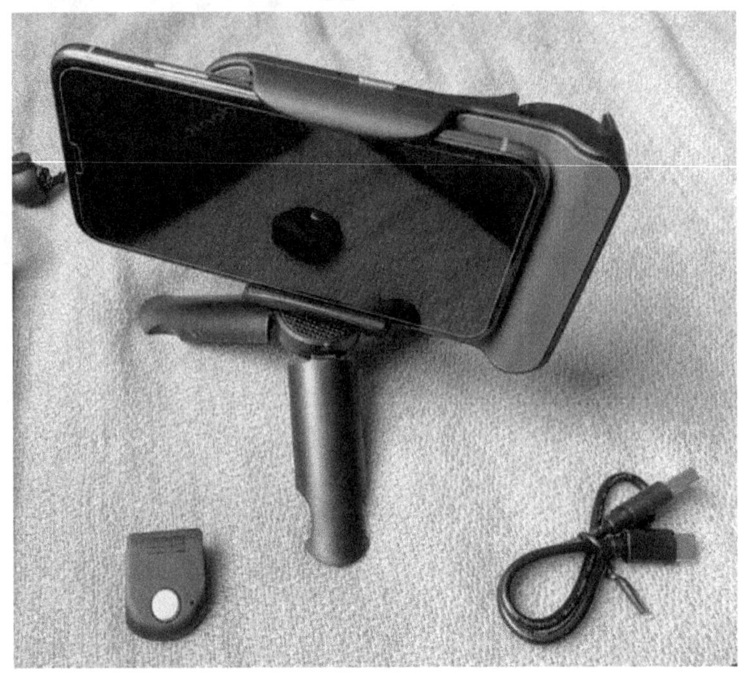

o **Beast grip**: Provides users with the opportunity to attach many types of standard conversion lenses, filters, photos, and even video accessories and gear. In addition, it adds stability and ease for handheld shots. The beast grip also provides users easy access to their phone buttons, USB and charging ports, superb design with a removable lens mount assembly and handle'.

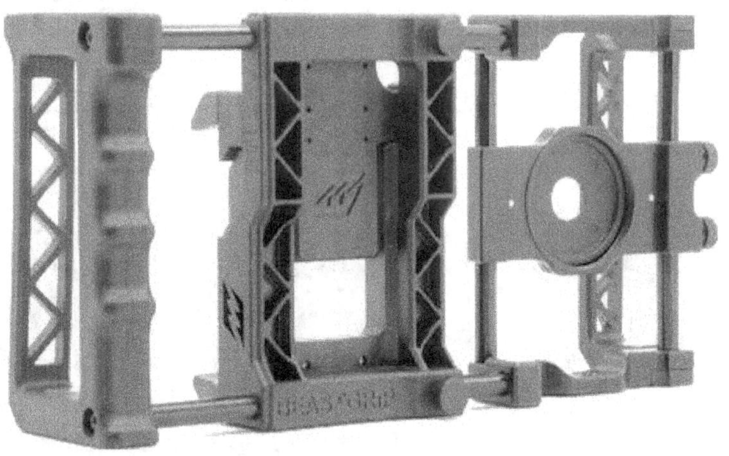

o **Lumu power**: The Lumu is a light meter version on our Smartphones. This device will turn your iPhone into a handheld light and color meter. Lumu works on any iPhone with a lightning port. Connect the Lumu to your gadget, and use it to adjust the lighting condition before taking that shot. The company that designed Lumu has now taken the game to another level. The new Lumu power now has two sides; the color side with a color sensor that measures the color temperature of the camera, white balance and illumination, and another side with a silicone photodiode that measures camera exposure, ambient light, and the flashlight.

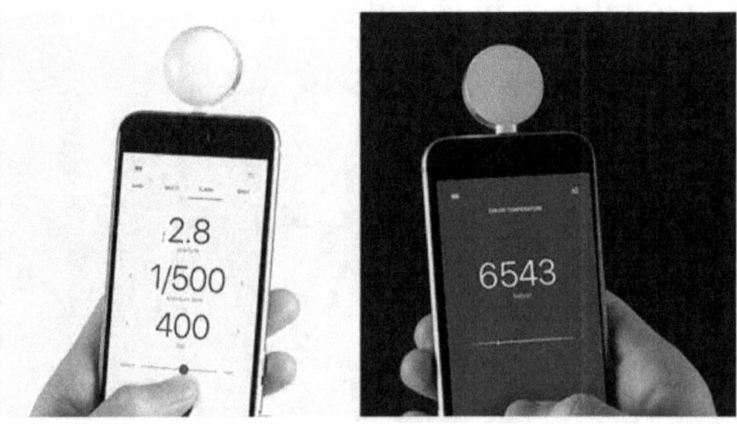

o **Dimmable selfie light with tripod**: this selfie light removes all the shadows from your video and makes the video looks more cine-matic. The tripod stand provides convenience for the users during video shooting.

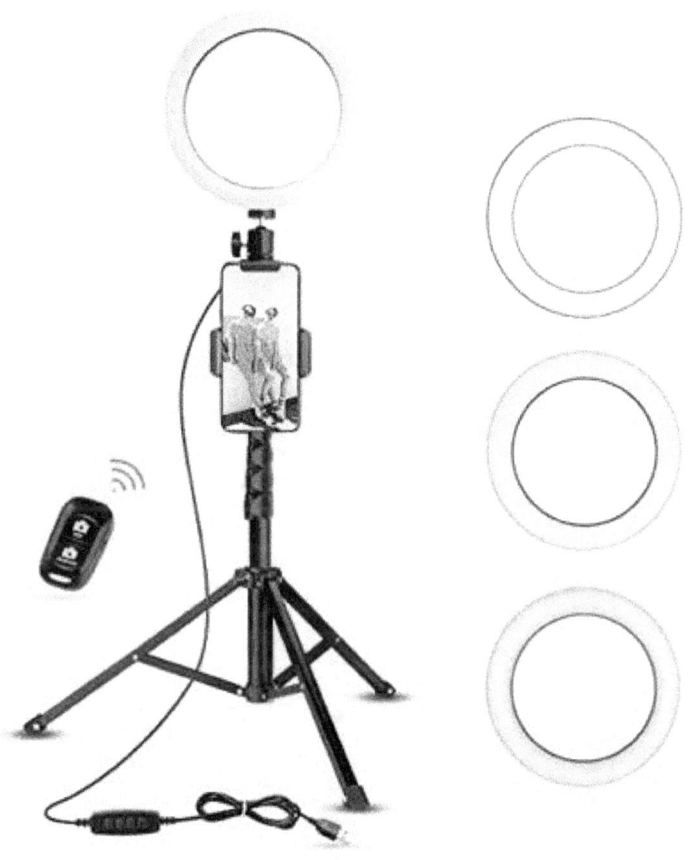

o **Underwater photographer case for iPhone SE**: iPhones are designed to be able to spend some time while in water either for a few minutes or second. If you want to take that cinematic shot while you are still under-water, this photographer case has got you covered. With this photographer case, you can safely take your phone deep inside the water, even beyond the depth advised by the manufacturers. The case protects your device from any underwater obstruction, and your lens is sure to give you a clear shot of everything.

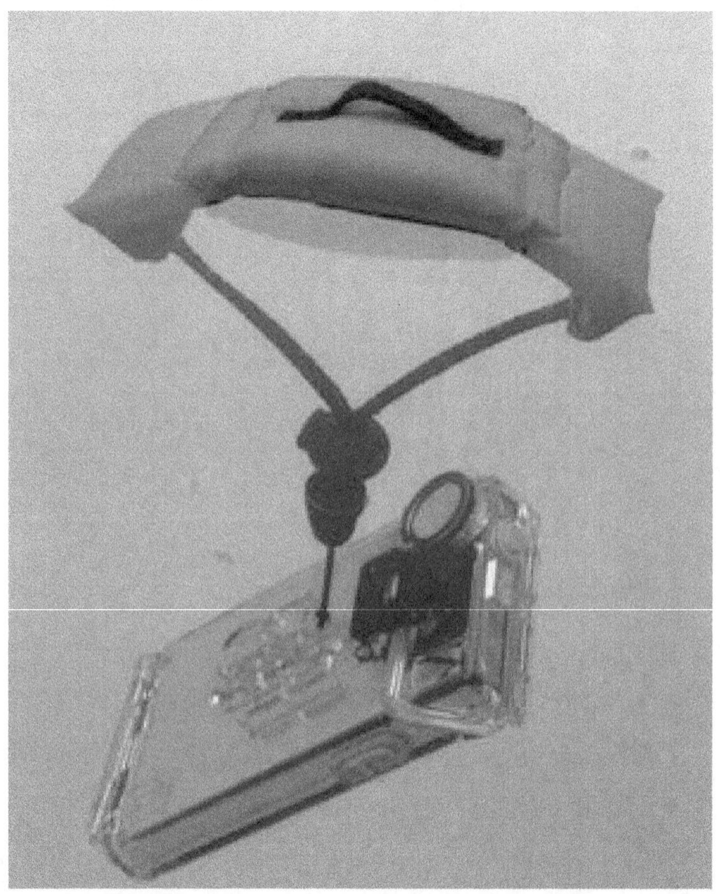

o **Tripod**: This is used to get the sharpest shot possible by positioning your phone camera at a better angle of the shooting. The Joby Gorillapod hybrid is ubiquitous and durable.

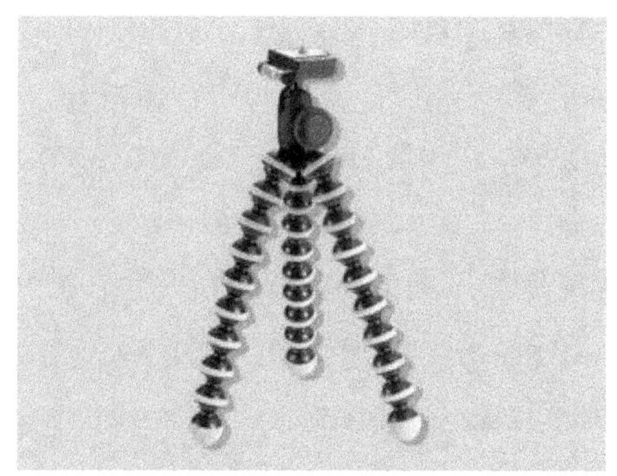

- **Rov Motorized Slider**: allows you to capture cinematic movements with your device. By just pressing a button, ROV will start moving and recording your videos seamlessly.

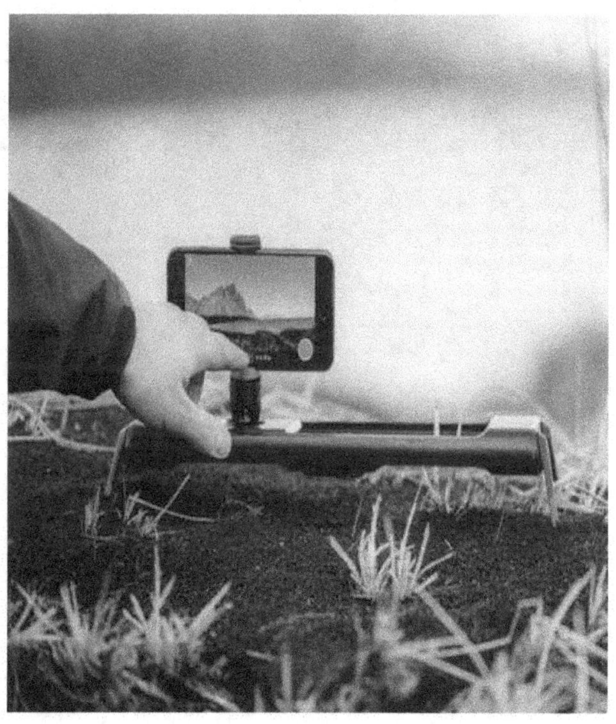

o **Profoto C1 plus cover**: This is an external flashlight that can sync with your iphone giving you access to control light anyhow you deem fit. The Profoto comes with an app that is only accessible with iPhones. The app comprises a camera function that can connect directly with the flash of the C1 plus. The Profoto serves as an improvisation to the LED light in the phone camera.

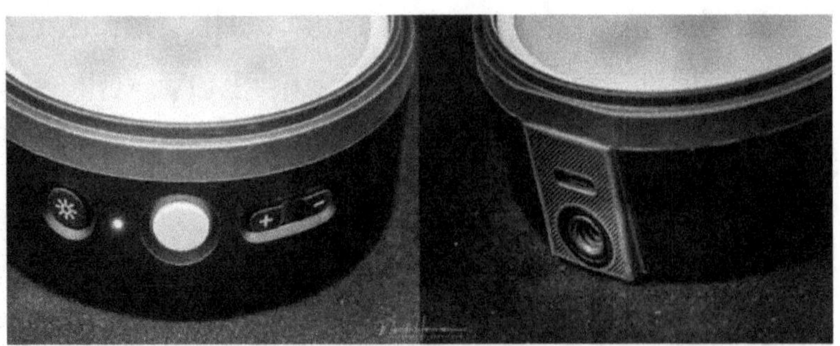

Chapter 4

HOW TO CONFIGURE FILMING SPEED ON THE iPhone SE 2020

In a bid to get almost everything done for users, Apple has a variety of filming speed that came with iPhones. Users have the liberty to select any filming gear that they want.

- You can choose any filming speed on the newly released iphone SE 2020 by tapping on camera from the settings.
- Choose the recording video mode to start recording and select from the available filming speed.

Alternatively, you can speed up your recorded video or speed it down with your iphone. The slow-motion recording mode in the iphone helps to shoot video in slow motion. There are two ways of achieving speed effect on iphone;

1. Install dedicated apple application on your device, which can let you speed up video previously recorded in normal mode. An excellent app for this is the free apple iMovie available online.
2. You can also speed up video recorded in Slo-Mo directly by speeding the Slo-Mo video back to average speed.

- Speeding up a video recorded in normal mode

- Download and install the iMovie app from the apple store.
- Start the app and navigate to the project section of the app.
- Click on the "+" sign to record a new movie.
- When the new project pops up, click on the movie tab.
- Locate the video that you want to speed up from normal mode, and click on the video.
- Click on the 'create movie' icon at the bottom of your screen.
- A video editing page will load, where you will have access to varieties of video editing tools.

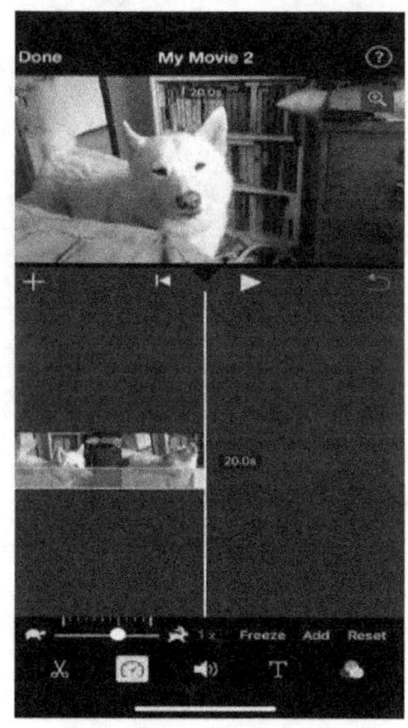

- Toggle the button that looks like a speedo-meter. That is the speed button.

- Start dragging the slider toward the right-hand side.

- The farther you shift the slider, the faster the video starts playing. The playing mode is now 2X, the former.

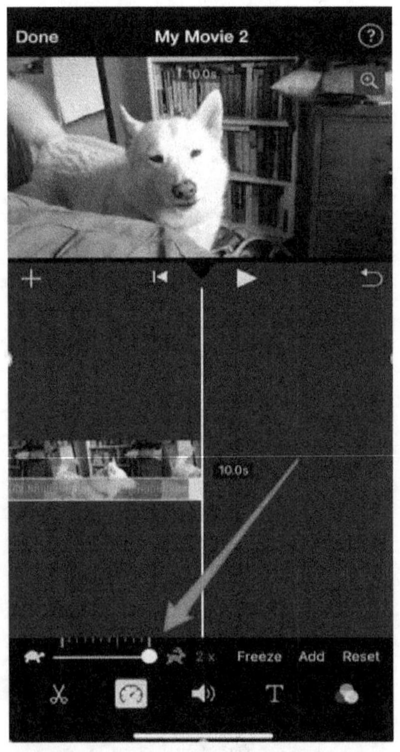

- Tap Done at the upper left corner of the screen to finish.

How to Speed up Video Recorded in Slo-Mo Back to Normal

Choose the Photos app from your device, and choose "Albums" at the bottom of your screen.

- Click on "Slo-Mo" to see the group of videos you had previously taken in slow motion, then select a video that you want to speed up.

- Select "Edit" at the top of your screen.

- Check the video timeline at the bottom of the screen. The tightly spaced dashes represent the regular speed video, while bits that are further apart represent the rest of the video in slow motion.

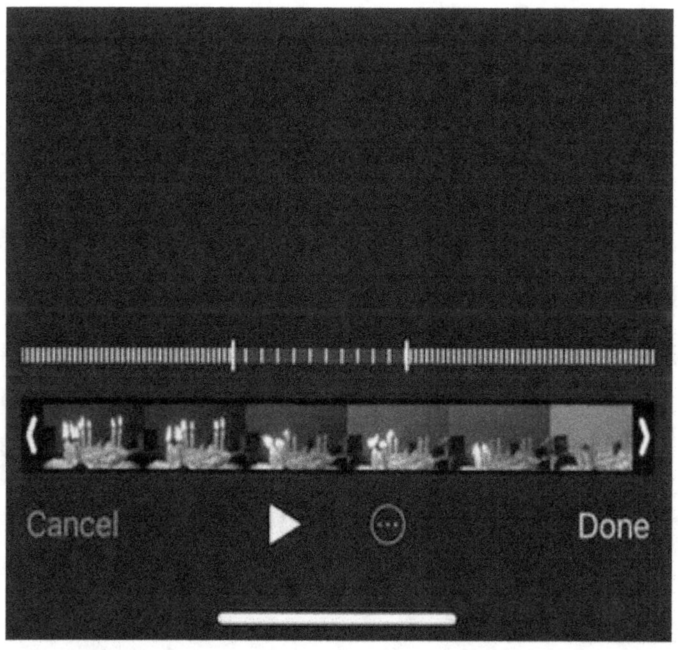

How to adjust color while shooting video on iPhone SE 2020

With the aid of the Filmic Pro app, which can be purchased online, you can vary the color temperature of your video shooting. You can take over the control of color temperature and tint inside the camera app. Each icon at the bottom of the screen represents different color temperature measured in kelvin. Let us look at the uses of the various symbols in color variation.

- The light bulb icon: this describes tungsten lighting or indoor shooting situation. Used to shoot indoor under low light.

- Sunlight icon: this represents natural sunlight. Choose this icon when you want to shoot during the day. The color temperature is about 6000k.

- Cloud icon: represents a cloudy condition. Used to shoot outdoor in the shade. The color temperature is about 6500k. Best use outdoor on a cloudy day.

- Fluorescent bulb icon: This represents the indoor lighting condition. Used to shoot in warehouse and office building. The color temperature is about 5500k.

Note: You can also decide to set your desired white balance preset by tapping on the A/B icon. Simply hold down on A until a window pops up.

The last icon is the AWB. This icon is capable of imitating whatever lighting condition you are at the moment and adjust the color accordingly.

You can change the tints by dragging down or dragging up the slider.

How to add a warped speed effect to your filming

Cinematographers usually add a warped result to films by using their camera. But this is equally achievable on the iphone. To add a wrapped speed effect to your filming, simply enable the Zoom wheel. The Zoom wheel, if activated, will allow you to apply the wrapped speed effect to your recording. Approach the subject slowly and turn the zoom wheel in the opposite direction against the actor.

Why you should add B-Rolls to your filming

B-roll is an act of storytelling. Sometimes, we might watch a 15minutes video only to get bored in the middle of the video. But some 3minutes videos seem interesting to us sometimes. See here, and it is not about the video length; it is about how each creator creates their stories. A B-roll is the additional part of the video that tells the viewers exactly what's going on in the background. Videographers need not necessarily add a B-roll, but adding them makes the story look real and engaging. You don't want a situation where your viewers get bored before the movie ended. B-roll might be necessary to create dramatic tension or further illustrate the point you're trying to make in your video. Examples of B-roll can include; shots of animate/inanimate objects that are not part of the story, shots directed at the atmosphere, a scene of the market e.t.c.

What can you achieve with a B-roll?

There are various ways you can use your B-roll footages;

- Douse tensions

- Establishing other facts that are not in the story.

- Covering up some errors in the A-roll footage.

How then can we shoot a perfect B-roll?

1. **Plan it**: figure out the how, why, and the when of your footage. You might do well to capture the entrance and exit of the president's office if

you're interviewing the president in his office. Create a plan of what you must do, when you need to do them and how to do them.

2. **Know the location beforehand:** your B-roll site might be a dark place where you will need to make proper adjustments to the camera. If you know this before you go there, you will know the right materials to take along to have a perfect shot.

3. **Shoot as many as possible B-roll:** you never know when you will need to remove a particular B-roll just to insert another one. Shooting as many as possible B-roll will give you many options to choose from.

4. **Get varied camera angles:** camera angle has a lot to do with the way your final work will look like. Choosing the right corner for your shot will imply a quality video at the end.

Different Camera Movements During Shooting

Experimenting with several cinematographic movements will add quality and visual appeal to your video.

- **Zooming:** is the most commonly used camera movement among videographers. It is often used as a grasp when the videographer doesn't know what other things to do to increase viewers' engagement with a shot. Deploy sometimes in your video to increase appeal. Zoom in or out from an unexpected, but very important, material or person in your video. Use a quick zoom to add life to a fast-paced piece and invigorate it.

- **Panning Camera Movement:** This involves changing the direction your camera is facing. Sometimes used to let viewers see more of the location where the video is being shot. The camera direction is aligned horizontally while switching between the left and right positions. The camera's view doesn't change, just the course that is changing.
- **Tilting:** This involves vertically moving the camera from up to down or down to up. The camera is mounted on a tripod as its angle is changing with each vertical motion.

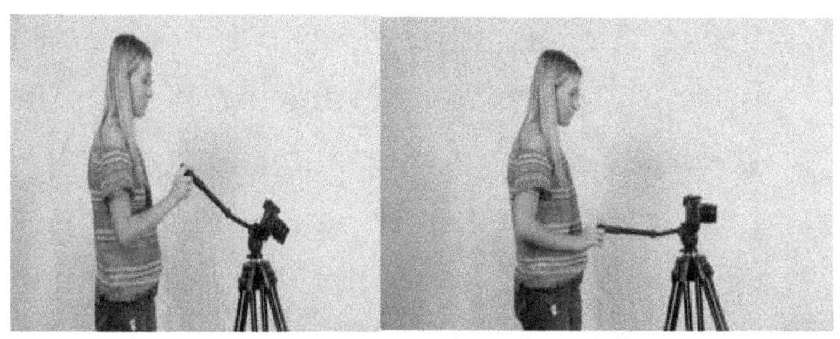

Tilting 1 and tilting 2

- **Dollying:** This is a type of camera movement that involves moving the whole camera in the forward and backward direction, using a track or motorized equipment. For active dolly movement, ensure your track is okay, and it allows fluidity of movement.

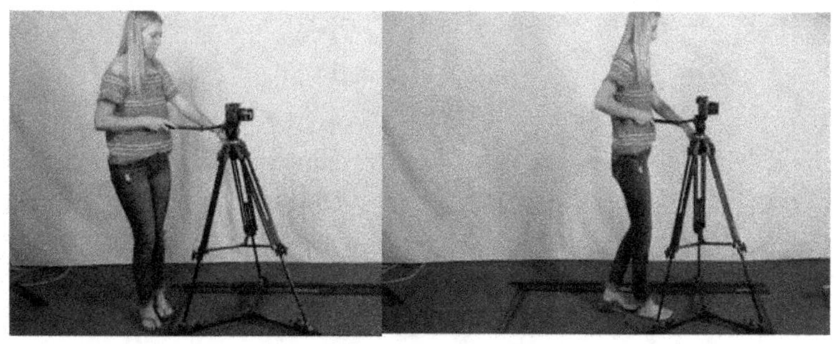

Dolly forward 1 and dolly forward 2

- **Trucking:** This is similar to dollying. The only difference is that camera movement is from left to right, unlike dollying.

- **Pedestal camera movement:** Involves moving your camera vertically up or down while it is mounted in a fixed position. This means we can always switch between two forms of pedestal movement: pedestal up, which denotes "moving the camera up;" and pedestal down, which means "moving the camera down." It is not the lens you are tilting up in this case; it is the entire camera undergoing the vertical motion. Just like when your camera is on a tripod, and you're only raising or lowering the tripod head.

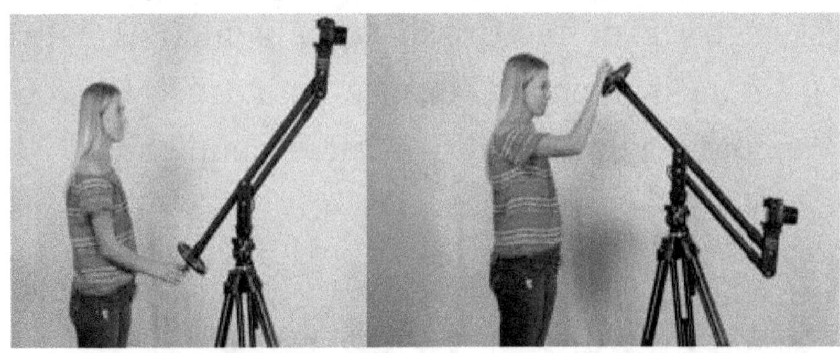

- **Handheld shooting:** Used when the action is moving very fast that attaching the camera to a tripod stand might not work, and you need to make the camera more mobile to be able to adjust to the action. The camera operator will hold the camera in his hands and may be required to switch between different camera movements such as dollying, trucking, panning, etc.

- **Crane:** you can use a crane when you want to reveal different things from different angles. It can be deployed to lift a considerable weight camera with the operator from a low position to a high position.

Benefits of Using External Lenses on the iPhone SE to Shoot Videos

When you incorporate additional lens to your iphone SE, you want to improve the way the subject in your shot looks like. Apple has been known for its consistent improvement in its product camera. But you can still get much more cinematic appeal from your iPhone SE camera – just by attaching a lens to the camera.

iPhone Lenses

Let us take a look at what the various type of glasses that are compatible with iPhone SE 2020 can help you to achieve;

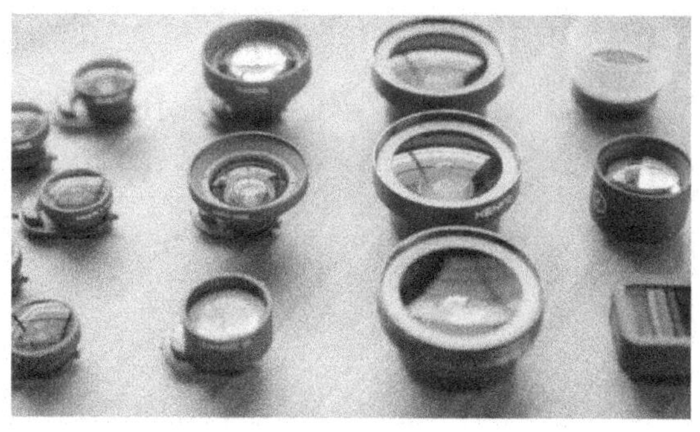

- **Wide-angle lens:** when you attach a lens like this to your iPhone, you will get a massive field of view. While shooting a scene with your iPhone camera, it might be challenging to move a step backward. You need not worry as you can achieve this with a lens attached to your device. It allows you to capture more of the entire location in the landscape to make a better view.

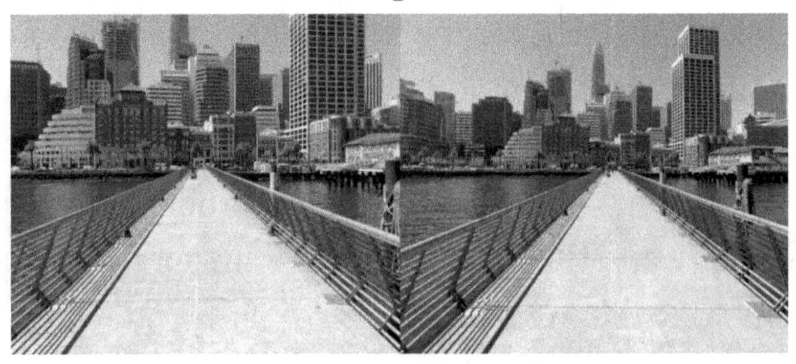

- **Telephoto lens:** This is much like when you are using digital zooming on your device. Digital zooming involves pinching out on your phone camera, thereby taking out a tiny portion of the image and stretching it. But digital zooming on your iPhone often leads to a blurry image, and this is why you might probably need a telephoto lens.

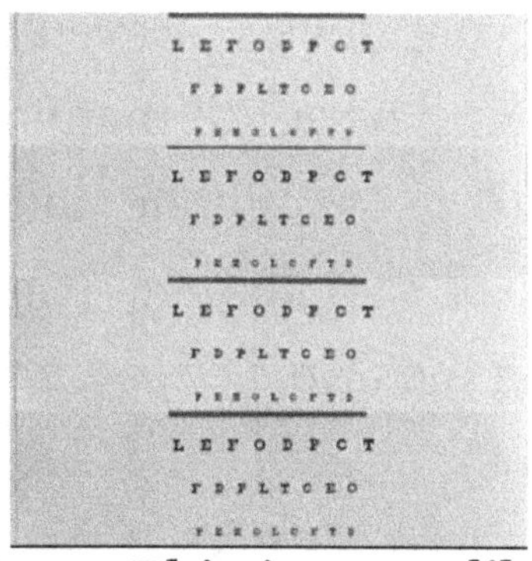

- **Macro lens:** This is more like a magnifying glass, allowing you to close up on a very small object.

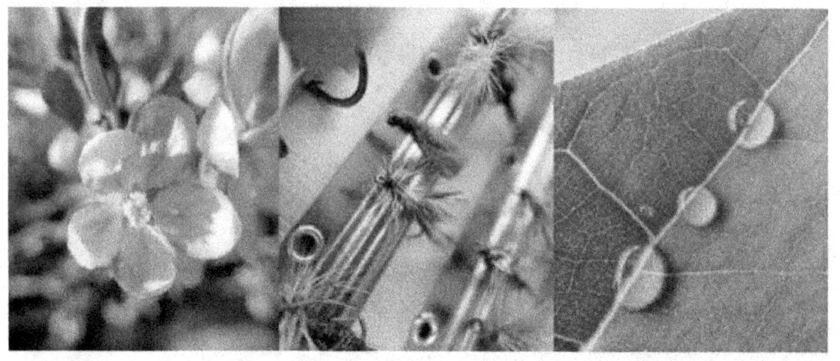

See those insects shot at a very far distance with a macro lens

One good reason for incorporating external lenses in your device is that you can easily leverage on it to give you freedom of movement and come up with a better shot appealing to viewers.

Adding audio effect on the iPhone SE video

You can add a variety of sounds to your videos in the iPhone. The sound can be any song you've downloaded on your device or even any other audio recording on your device. All that you need to do is to download iMovie for iPhone and then install it. After you finished installation, you can carry out any of these with the iMovie app on your iPhone.

a. *Adding songs using iMovie on your iPhone:* follow these simple steps on the iMovie app.

- Open your projects in the iMovie timeline, and click on which is the 'Add media button'.
- Select Audio, and choose any of the options below;
  - Tap soundtrack icon to allow you to browse the inbuilt soundtrack

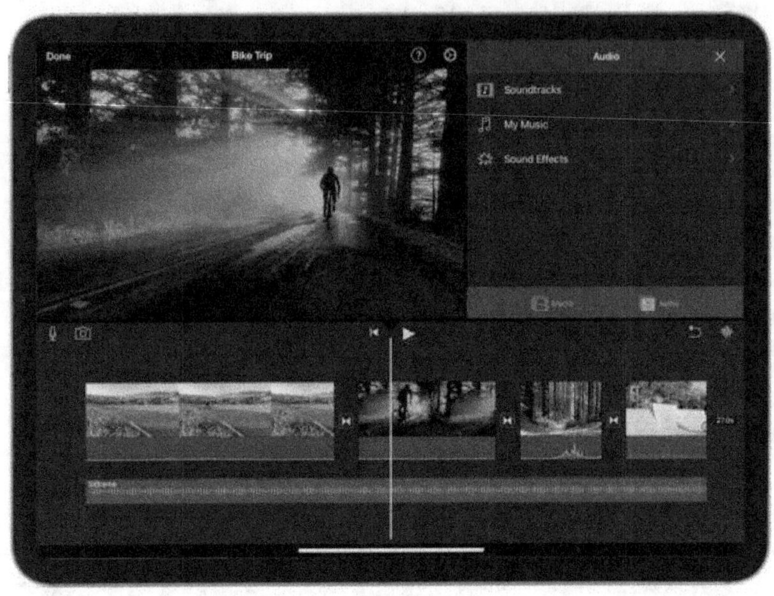

- Click on 'my music' to explore previously downloaded music on your iPhone.

- Tap 'my music >> file' to browse songs saved on your iCloud.

- You can click on any song you wish to add just to preview once more before adding.

- Tap the + icon next to the song to add it to your project.

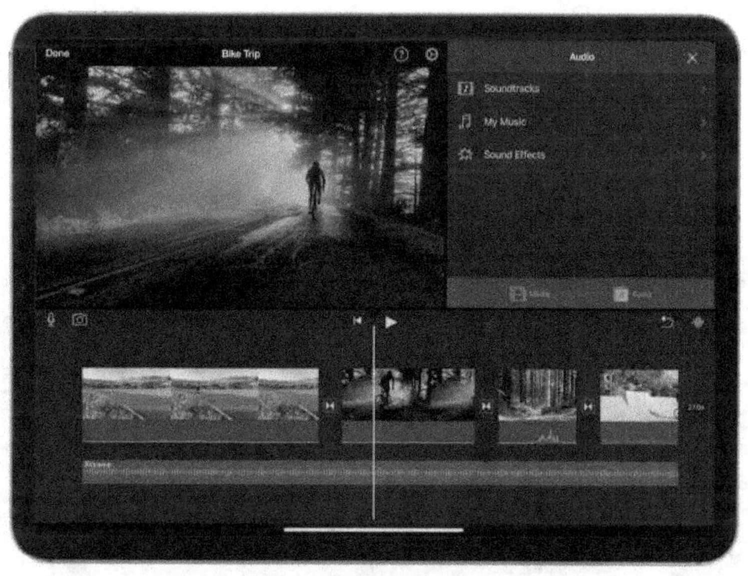

Adding songs using iMovie on iPhone

b. **Adding a sound effect in iMovie on the iPhone.**

- Open your project on iMovie, and scroll your timeline so that a white vertical line will appear just where you want to add the sound.

- Click on add media button>audio>options:

    a. Click on 'sound effect' to explore the built-in sound effect you already have on the app.

    b. Click on my music to explore the sound effect in your music file.

    c. Click on 'file' to explore songs in your iCloud.

- You can preview any song you want to add by tapping on it.

- Tap the add effect button .to add the sound effect to your video

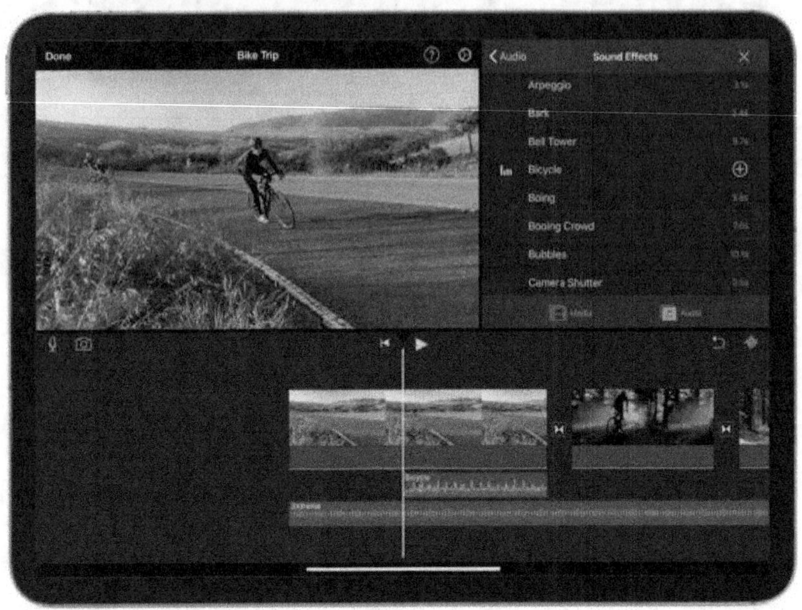

Shooting 4k videos at 60fps for YouTube with the iPhone SE, Tips and tricks

Before we talk about the tips and tricks to shoot the best possible 4k video on your iPhone SE 2020, let us check how we can even access the 4k 60fps video mode from the camera.

a. Tap open the camera app on your iPhone SE 2020.

b. Click on video.

c. Having launched the video mode, click on the resolution to switch between 4k mode and full HD mode.

d. Click on the frame rate icon to see the list of available fps.

e. Choose the 60fps.

Note:

- 4k at 24 fps is the recommended for cinematic video. It delivers 135MB worth of space per minute.

- 4k at 30 fps delivers 170MB worth of space, and it is of high resolution.

- 4k at 60 fps will deliver 400MB per minute. The resolution is higher and smoother.

Tips for shooting

- Stabilize your footages to avoid shaky videos. You can use gimbal for this purpose.
- Use precise lighting conditions for your footage to avoid overexposed background or underexposed actors.
- Apply color grading to your footage.

How to shoot foreground videos

There are three layers of shot compositions; foreground, middle ground, and the background. Having a shallow depth of field in your shot can be that one chance to introduce quality in your video. Shooting in the foreground is when the object/ subject very close to your camera is brought into a focus, and everything in the background appears blurred out. If you're using a real camera, you can have a shallow depth of field by just adjusting your camera's aperture. But you cannot manually control the depth of field using an aperture in iPhone because the iPhone camera doesn't have an aperture.

The iPhone's AE/AF lock function can enable you to adjust your camera's depth of field. You can just press and hold on your camera screen while the subjects/actors you want to capture are in the foreground. Pressing and holding on the camera screen will lock the focus on the subject and blur everything in the background, enhancing your subject.

How to shoot creative shots from different angles

There are a variety of ways you can capture your shots creatively from different angles. You don't just stay in one place and imagine you can come up with nice shots. You need to change position and know the one that can give you leverage to shoot a better video.

Here are tips to enable you to take a very good shot while experimenting with different angles of shooting.

- **Capturing from a low side:** shooting from a low angle is advisable if you want the subject in your shot to appear bigger than it ordinarily was. A low angle gives a shallow field of depth, and it adds more details about the foreground in your shot.

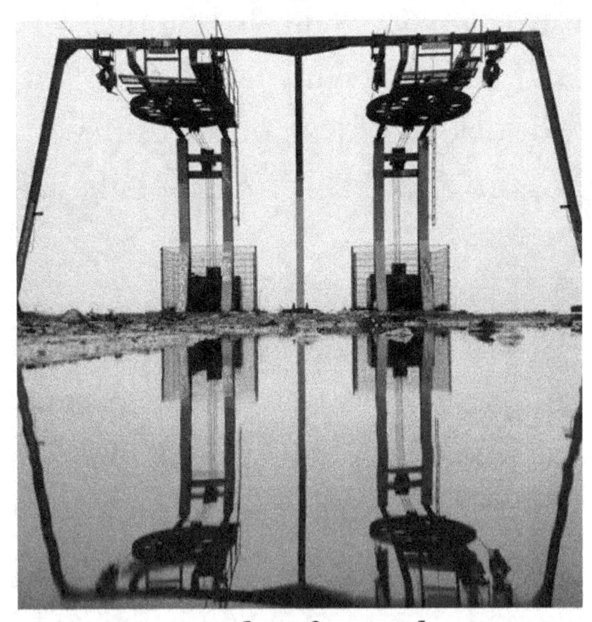

The above image was shot from a low camera angle. The image was located at the center of a town, and the whole town as the background has been removed, leaving only the sky in the background. You can creatively shoot from a low angle to remove unnecessary items in the background.

- **Taking a shot from a high vantage point**: When the video-grapher takes a shot from a vantage, it makes the actor looks smaller than they are in relation to the environment where the image was shot. The image below was shot from a vantage. Look at how small the subject is in relation to what is in the surrounding.

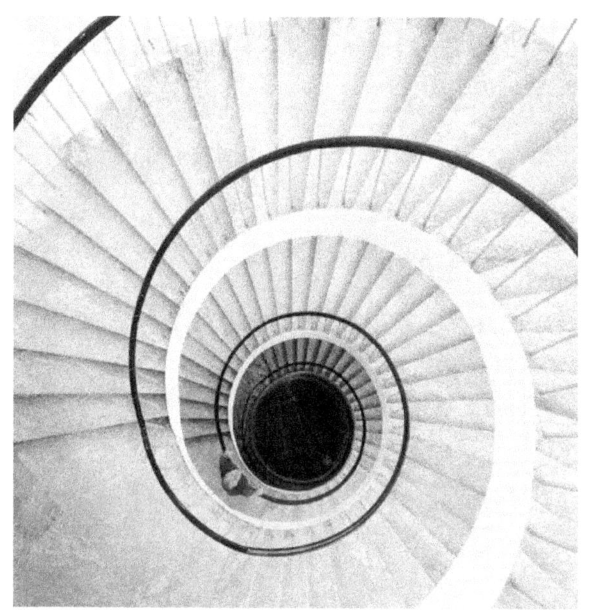

- **Capturing shots from a high angle:** by shooting higher like the one below, you can leverage the ground as your beautiful background.

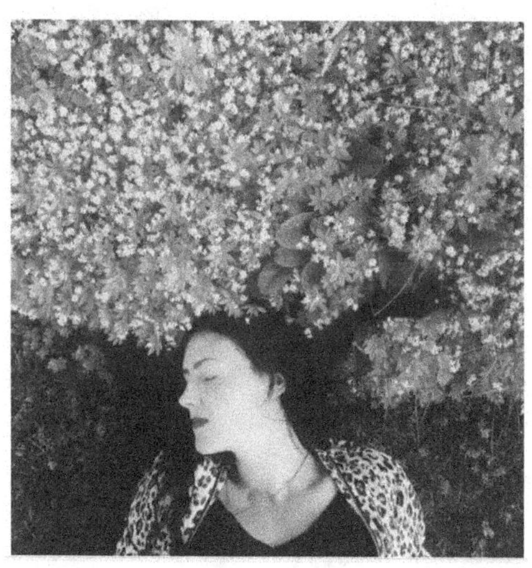

- **Choosing different height:** Rather than taking your shots from the same level all the time, why not experiment with different heights and see what works better. You can even bring an air of suspense in your shot by taking pictures of subjects from behind.

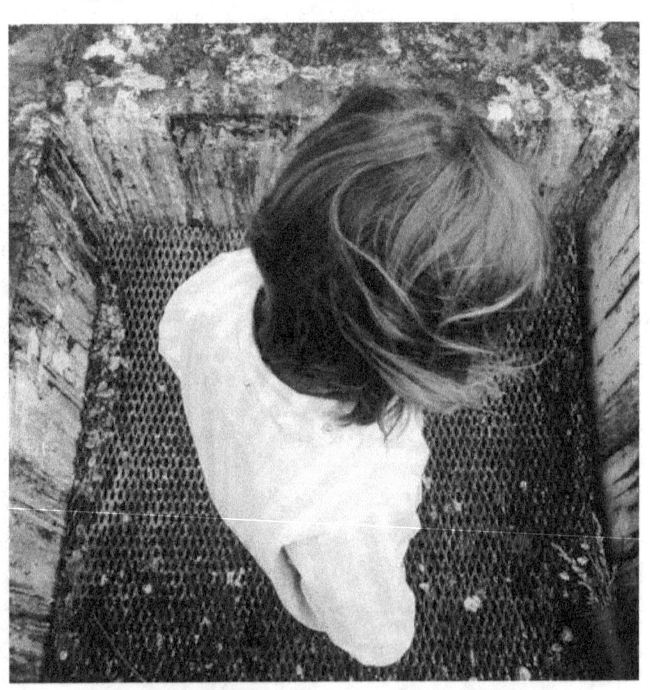

Chapter 5

Using FilMic Pro App for Cinematic Shots on the iPhone SE 2020

Downloading and installing the FilMic pro app is no rocket science. All that it takes is your data. Because there are websites online, where you can download it for free. Go to the app store and search Filmic pro. It will load and bring the app to the interface for you. Click on 'get' and start downloading. After downloading, go back to your device and click on the app to start the installation processes. You will be prompted so many times to allow the app to continue taking response from your camera app, audio, video, microphone, etc. You can also visit *app.app-valley.vp*, and download it for free.

Setting up FilMic Pro

Your iPhone SE does not come with any particular manual, telling you exactly how to get the most out of your device. There are several third-party apps that can be installed on your device. These apps can allow you to have control of some manual settings which do not ordinarily accompany your gadget. One such app that has become widely used is the

FilMIc pro, which provides you with cutting-edge settings to get the best out of every shot you take with your device. The iPhone SE 2020 is compatible with the FilMic pro app, so you don't need to worry about compatibility. Having securely installed your FilMic pro app from a trusted source, the next is to start using the app to achieve creative shots. Check the following content to see how to exhaustively utilize all the functions that accompanied FilMic pro.

The FilMic Pro Interfaces and Menus

The interfaces in the FilMic pro apps are the features users can explore to get the best use of their camera app. See below for the menus that come with the app;

- **The Main Menu**

  Click the settings icon on the app to have access to the main menu functions;

Tapping the settings icon will bring all the menus as it is shown below;

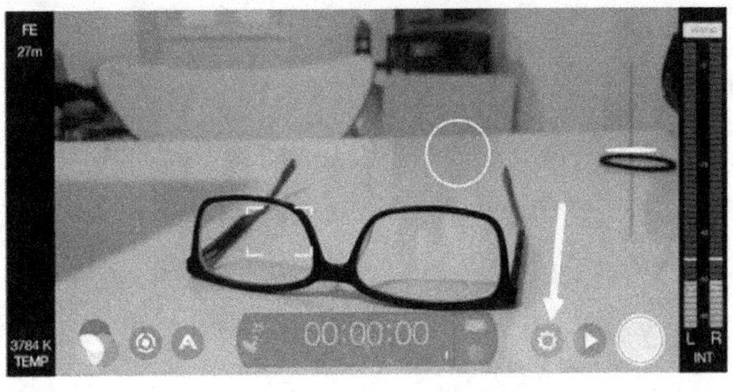

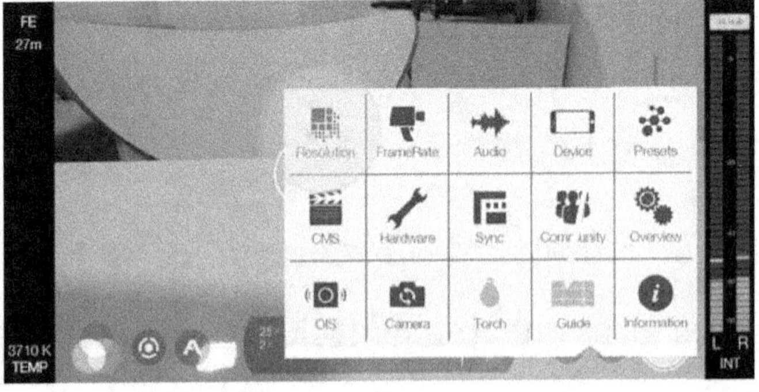

Now that we have seen the menus, let us take a look at the features one after the other.

Resolution menu

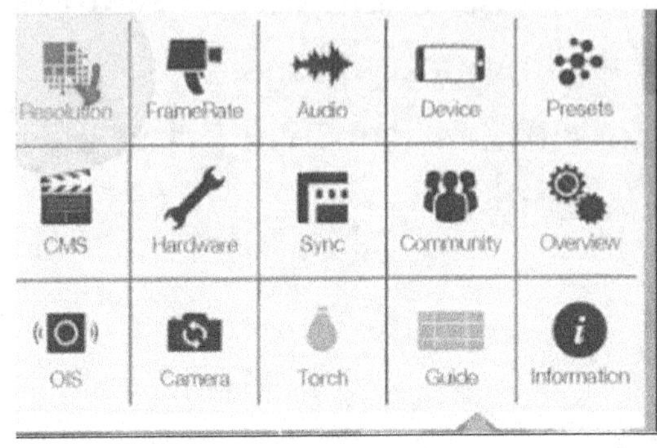

Once you tap on the resolution icon above, the section below where you can choose any resolution of choice will pop up.

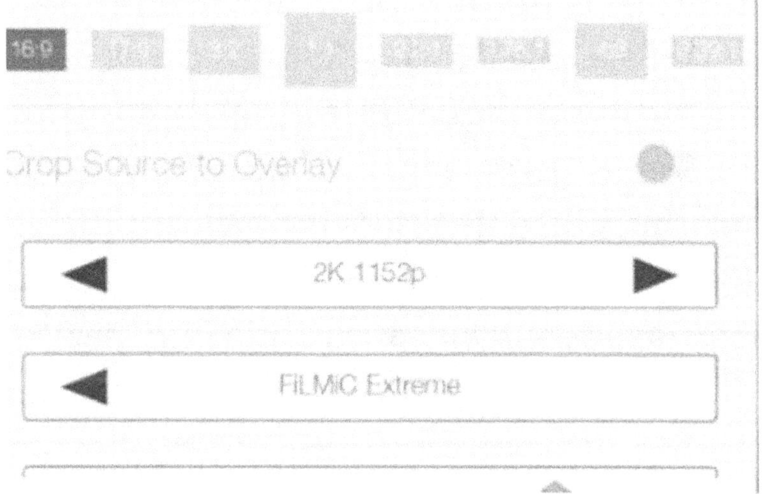

As an iPhone SE 2020 user, the following resolutions are available; 4k 2160p, 3k 1836p, 2k 1152p, HD 1080p and HD 720p. The best resolution for most of your cinematic shootings is the 2160 4k. This resolution gives moderate shots with high quality. You can as well adjust the recording quality (bitrate). The bit rate also determines the camera's recording quality. You can choose between different bit rates. The available bit rates include FilMic Extreme, FilMic quality, apple standard, and Economy. Each bit rate signifies different recording quality for your shot.

- For the **FiLMiC Extreme**, the FilMic pro app sets a value of 100mbps for 2k, 3k, and 4k, respectively. While at 1080p, the target is 50mbps. The FilMic Extreme is the highest you can choose, and produce an enormous file size.

- For the **FiLMiC quality**, the standard is 32mbps at 1080p for users to improve image quality, detail of the image, and the color information.

- For the **Apple Standard**, you will get the same Mbps as you get with the conventional cameras

- The **Economy** comes with lower resolution and consumes less space.

From the resolution settings, you can also select the aspect ratio from the list of available aspect ratios. The list of available aspect ratios you can get from the FilMIc pro are; 16:9, 17:9, 3:2, 1:1, 2.2:1, 2.76:1, 4:3, and 2.39:1. Most videos are shot with the 16:9 aspect ratios. The 16:9 aspect ratio is the standard mostly convenient on your iPhones, TVs, and other gadgets. When you want to use other aspect ratios that are not the normal 16:9, you need to switch off the 'crop overlay source.'

The Frame rate menu

The Frame rate or Frames per Second is the exact number of frames the camera captured or played back in a second timeframe. Choosing high frame rates implies creating a bigger file size, which requires high processing power. However, a high fps doesn't necessarily mean your video is of higher quality video.

The frame rate mode selector, which is located at the top right corner of the screen, will allow you to switch between the Standard and Timelapse mode. The top section of the frame rate menu gives you the displays of the 'standard' frame rate presets that your device can support. The default Preset options that you can choose from include: 24fps, 25fps, 30fps, 48fps, 50fps, 60fps, 120fps and 240fps. Clicking on any of these frame rates will leave a gray circle on it and will set your fps to any value you choose. The 24fps, 25fps, and the 30fps are the most common among seasoned videographers. The 24 fps and the 240 fps shown in lighter grey color are only available base on the resolution the user is using to shoot.

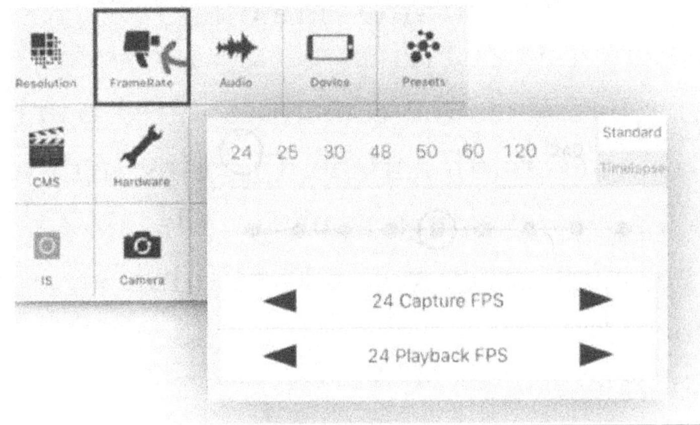

Audio settings

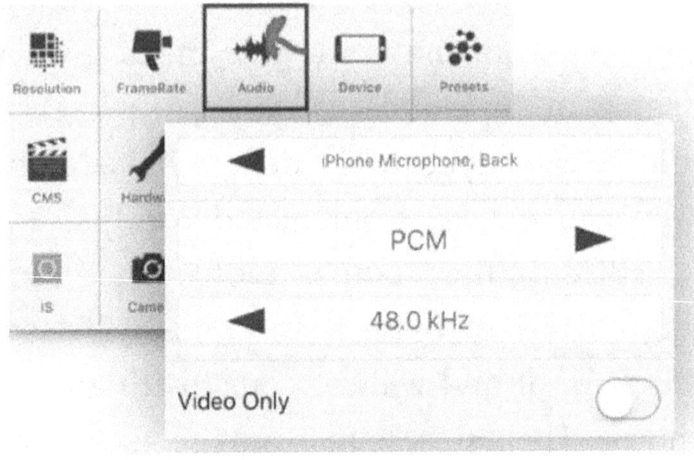

Device Settings

Tap the audio mode to activate the audio settings. This is where you will be able to decide if you want to add an external microphone or use your device microphone. An external microphone gives quality audio, so you should understand what you want. Don't toggle on the video only mode unless you want to start recording without sound. These are the list of microphone selection modes that you can select from; Video Only mode, iPhone Microphone (Bottom), iPhone Microphone (Front), iPhone Microphone (Back). The supported audio sampling rates are 44.1 kHz, 48 kHz, and 96 kHz. The 48 kHz is advisable.

Some additional audio options include;

Automatic Gain Correction – This is activated when the iPhone's inbuilt microphone is used or with an external microphone without any noticeable gain level adjustment. If you unchecked this setting on your iPhone, then it means you're using an external microphone that supports a native gain control on the microphone itself.

Voice Processing - When this setting is enabled, kindly highlights audio frequencies in the range of human speech to bring out the human voice better.

Bluetooth Audio Monitoring - (There is no on-screen switch in the app for this) you can connect Bluetooth headphones to your device using the Apple settings app under the Bluetooth heading.

When you connect Bluetooth headphones, the audio output is routed automatically to the Bluetooth device. It is only advisable to connect Bluetooth headphones when using the app. The use of a Bluetooth speaker could lead to a disruptive audio feedback loop as the microphone could pick up the speaker's audio output.

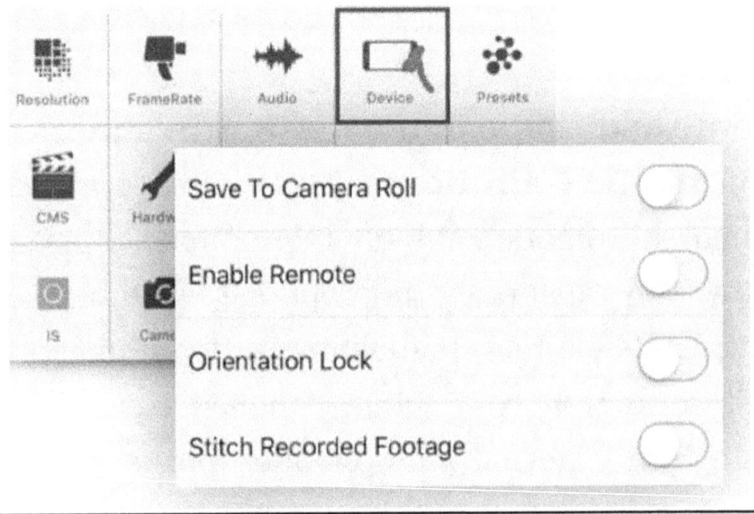

Let us talk about each icon one after the other.

- *Save to Camera Roll*: if you enable this setting, you can have your recordings saved by default to the camera roll. Note: the FiLMiC pro manufacturer advises users to employ the FiLMiC library to keep their recordings due to the following reasons: - the original video quality is guaranteed for users that use the FiLMiC library. – You can maintain the filename without any change to it. - Another concern is that the camera roll might sometimes fail the users. The data might be lost when copying to or saving the recordings to the camera roll.

- *Enable Remote:* You can enable this setting if FilMic remote has been linked with your FilMic app.

- *Orientation Lock:* This setting enables users to controls the ability to maintain the current orientation of the FilMic app. For instance: Enabling this setting while in the vertical orientation will keep the app locked vertically. On the other hand, if you enable this setting while in the landscape mode, the app will be maintained in a vertical orientation.

- *Stitch Recorded footage***:** during live recording, this mode will allow users to pause and resume their footage. The clips are later joined together.

How to save from FilMic Pro to the Camera Roll

- Tap the 'play button' to open the FilMic library.
- Click on the multi-clip selection icon.
- Tap each recording you want to save to the camera roll.

- Click the save to the camera roll button to save the recording.

- Wait for the confirmation indicating all recordings have been transferred.

Preset functions on FilMic Pro

The preset function allows users to initiate, save, and update presets for most of the app's settings. This allows users to remember a particular shooting technique they once used easily. If you want a customized Preset for your favorite Motion FX, you can select the desired fps and then save it as a Preset. You might also want to create your desired economy Preset especially when you don't have much storage left on your iPhone, select 720, choose a lower bit rate and save it as a Preset. The iOS data storage algorithm is not programmed to recognize symbols such as *&@, so do not use them to save your file.

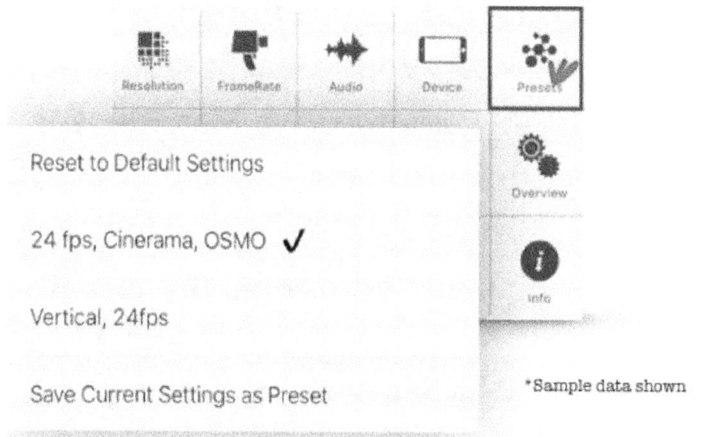

Content Management system (CMS) on FilmMic pro

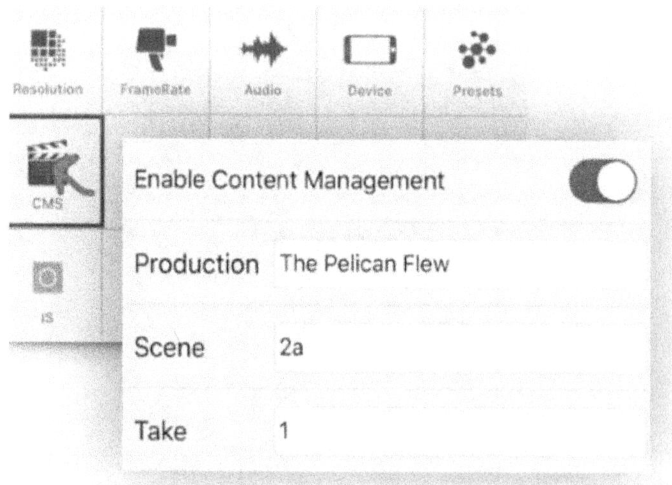

The CMS (Content Management System) settings, if enabled, can be used to control the file-naming algorithm of the FilMic pro app. The FilMic pro app is programmed to save your recordings using the date and time it was the recording was created. A filename '28052020_171425.mov' would imply that the video file was recorded on May 28, 2020, at 5:14 PM local time. But enabling the CMS setting will save the recording's filenames using a system of strings to show the Production, Scene, and Take of each footage.

- Production: You can set a general production name for this, which you will be using for all your recordings. You can change it later if you want.

- Scene: You can set a general scene name for this, which you will be using for all your recordings. You can change it later if you want

- Take: You can set a number to indicate the start of your work.

Hardware

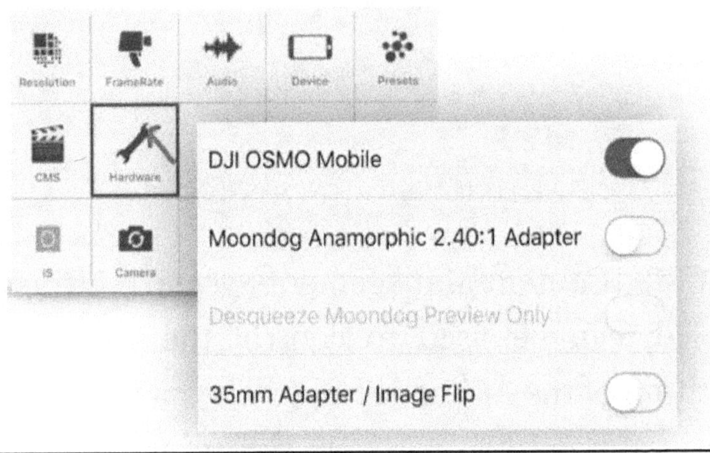

DJI OSMO Mobile: Users can leverage this button to control the FilMic pro app using the hardware buttons of a DJI OSMO Mobile handheld gimbal.

How to Connect your OSMO to FiLMiC Pro app: - Toggle on the Bluetooth on your iPhone, and make sure the Bluetooth is placed in your OSMO when the OSMO is switched on. – Enable the OSMO mobile in the hardware setting of the FilMic pro app. – A dropdown box will be prompted where you can select the OSMO you want to connect with. - The Bluetooth connection is then established.

Using the OSMO and FiLMiC Pro: - Utilize the four buttons available on the OSMO to control various FilMic pro menus: - **The circular joystick control. The shutter button** – This button is used as the mode selector. - **The record button** – use to either start or stop recordings. – **The trigger button**- Tap this button twice to reset OSMO's orientation.

Moondog Anamorphic 2.40:1 Adapter: Enables the FilMic app to be able to de-squeeze footage that was shot with the Moondog Labs Anamorphic Adapter.

Desqueeze Moondog Preview only: when enabled, can be used to de-squeeze video during the post-production. It provides a de-squeezed, 'finished' appearance for the video preview.

35mm Adapter / Image Flip: to ensure the video is the correct orientation when using a lens adapter.

Sync menu

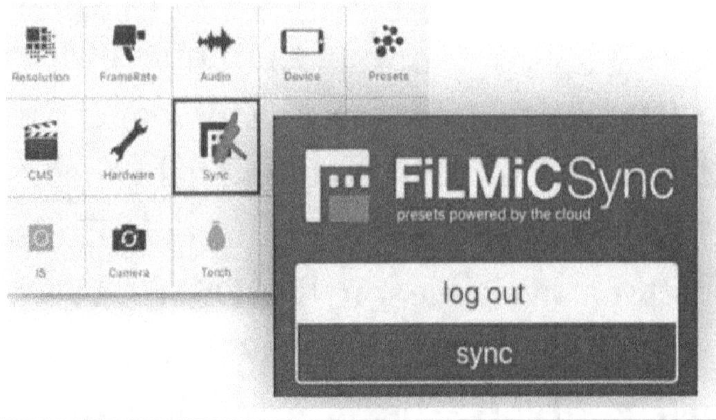

The FiLMiC Sync: offers users the chance to synchronize all of their preset data to a secured cloud storage account. You can even download your preset data with another device just by synchronizing your data for seamless access. This is very useful in the case of theft when your device gets missing. All your preset data can still be traced to another device.

To use FiLMiC Sync:

Click the signup button to begin a Sync account with your name and email. Or use your Facebook login to register.

Community

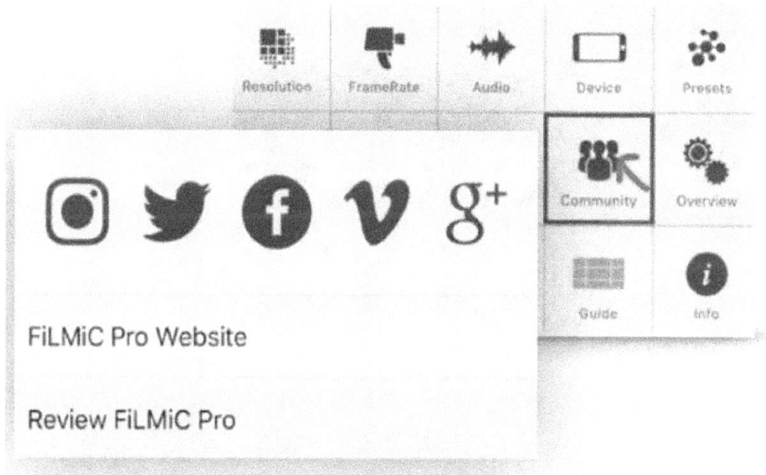

This is an avenue to connect with FilMic pro on any of their social media account. You can reach them via Facebook, Instagram, Twitter and other available platforms. You can reach out to their support desk in case of any technical issue you want to report.

Overview

You will be able to see all the current configuration the FilMic app is currently running on. It shows the frame rate, hardware in used, bit rate and the active screen resolution.

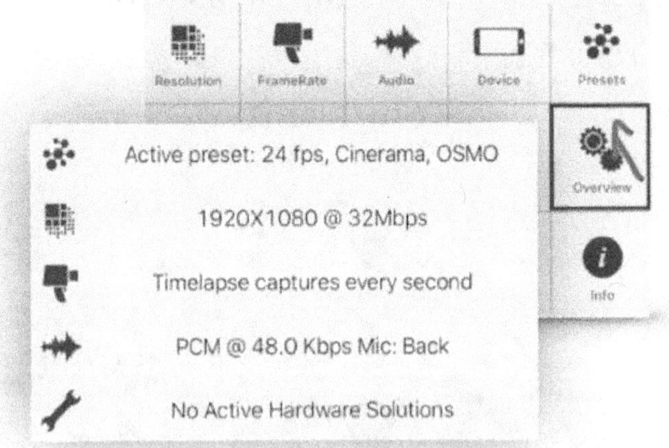

Image stabilization

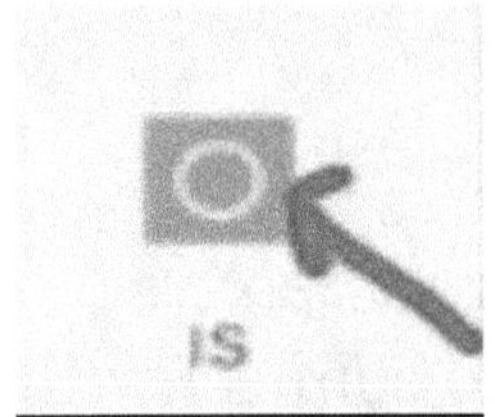

You can enable this if you don't have a tripod or a gimbal to stabilize your device. It provides a more steady footage when you are using your hand to shoot.

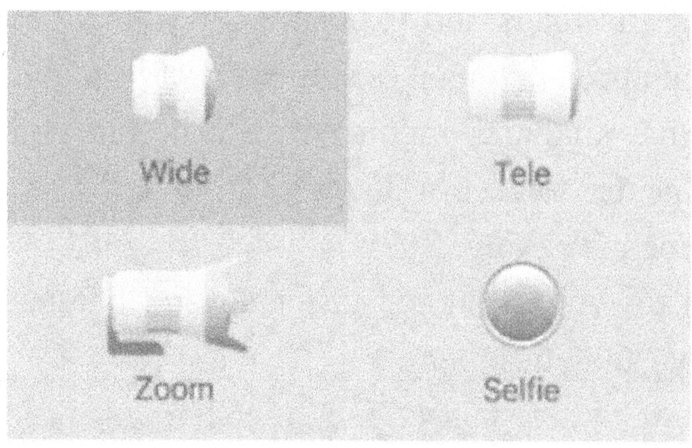

This multi camera setting is still in the making, and only work on iPhone 7 for now.

Guide

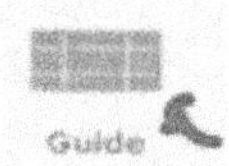

This serves to get the right framing for your shots.

Information

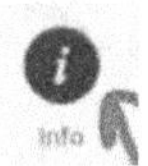

This icon contains important information for easy navigation of the FilMic pro.

To set the focus and exposure for your video, the FilMing pro app engages some sets of live analytics. The live analytics menu consists of four buttons which cater for Zebra Stripes, Clipping, False Color and Focus Peaking.

Press the **A** icon at the lower control bar to show the live analytics menu.

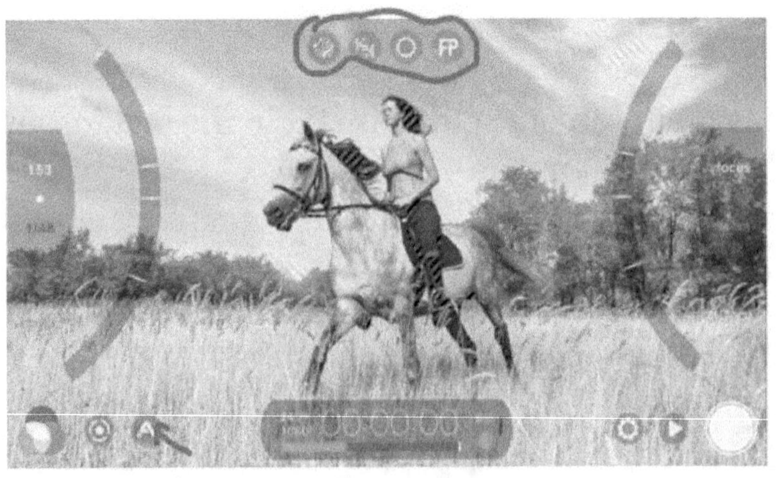

The four live analytic menus are shown in red circle above.

The zebra stripes set exposure by marking the image with red forward stripes(overexposure) and blue backward stripes(underexposure).

Clipping shows you the clipped area of exposure.

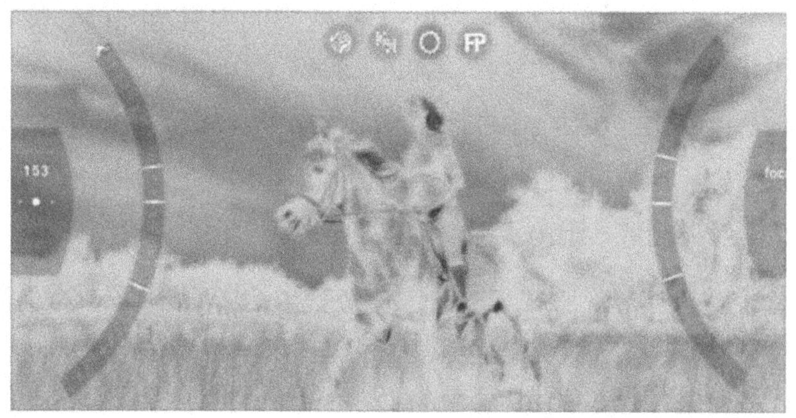

False color shows the full profile of the video exposure. Red indicates overexposure, while blue indicates underexposure.

Focus peaking: Light blue shows areas of focus and green shows that the subject is in critical focus.

Setting Gamma

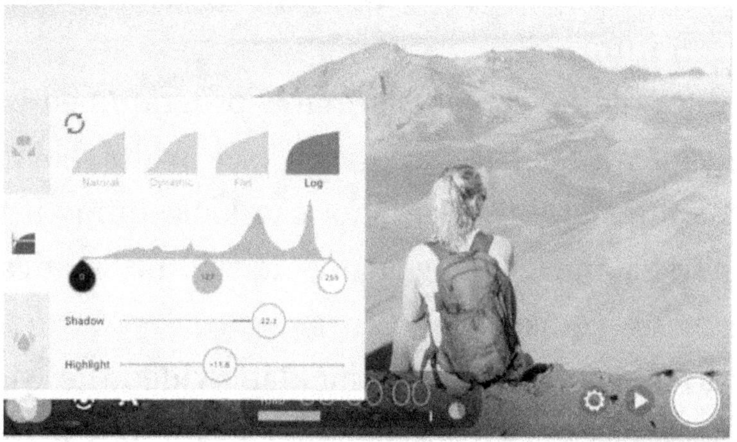

The top category of the Tone sub-panel has four gamma curve options that users can apply to their videos. There is the default tone which is based on the iPhone's default mode. Dynamic, Flat and Log curves are intended to allow for significant flexibility in tone and dynamic range. The log option is especially useful for professionals doing color grading, but it is prone to the possibility of increased noise or other noticeable errors. The Flat curve is recommended due to performance advantage.

Setting white balance

Setting white balance enables users to record colors as precisely as possible with their device's camera. Different light sources come with different color temperatures.

Modern digital cameras are now programmed with sensors which can accurately set white balance automatically. But your shot can look untidy if the white balance changes by itself automatically during the process.

So, to allow users shoot cinematic video the white balance has to be locked. You can initially set the white balance by holding a piece of white material in front of the camera.

You can set and lock the white balance in the FilMic app by clicking the colored circle icon at the bottom left of the interface.

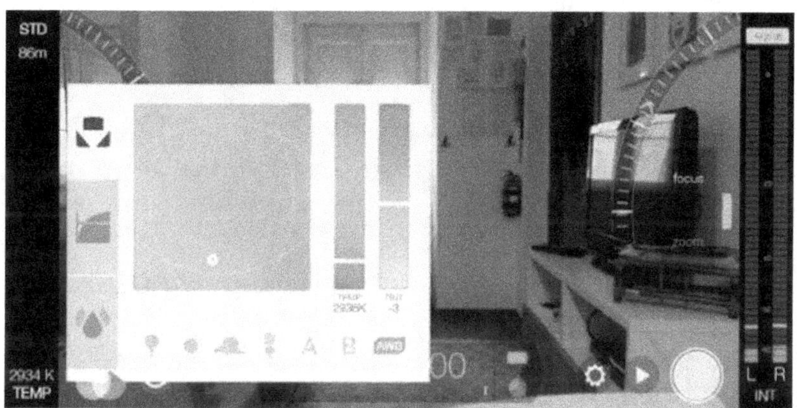

Selecting the AWB icon will automatically change the white balance as you move from one location to another location, of from one lighting condition to another.

The color menu

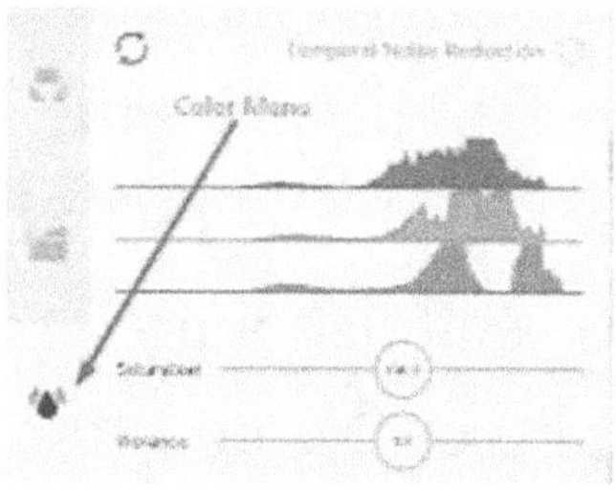

This menu gives you a good control of color.

You can have direct access to the manual controls through any of the following methods

- Long held any corresponding reticle to have access to either the focus control or the exposure control – Navigate between the right and the left side of the screen to open exposure or focus respectively.

- Navigate backward to dismiss the manual control and bring on the reticle.

-**Exposure**: you can adjust the exposure by changing the left arc up or down. This way you can change both the ISO and Shutter Speed.

- **ISO/Shutter Lock**: You can lock any specific value of the ISO or Shutter speed by clicking on the top or bottom of the app's exposure control block. In the picture below, the shutter has been locked at 1/48th. Locking one value allows the app to freely adjust the other through its range. ISO Priority You can use the control in between the ISO and Shutter displayed values to set the ISO priority range. In doing so you can establish a preferred range of ISO values you would like the app to stay within. This assists in maintaining a quality exposure and guard against ISO noise which can be common in shots with high ISO settings. Focus Adjust the focus by moving the right arc up or down. Note that on smart phones and tablets, the small lens is calibrated to focus to infinity in a short range.

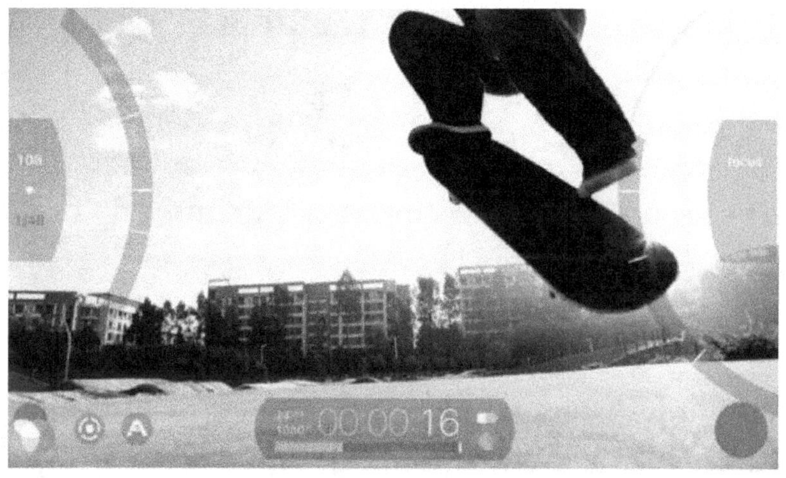

Recording Videos on the FilMic Pro

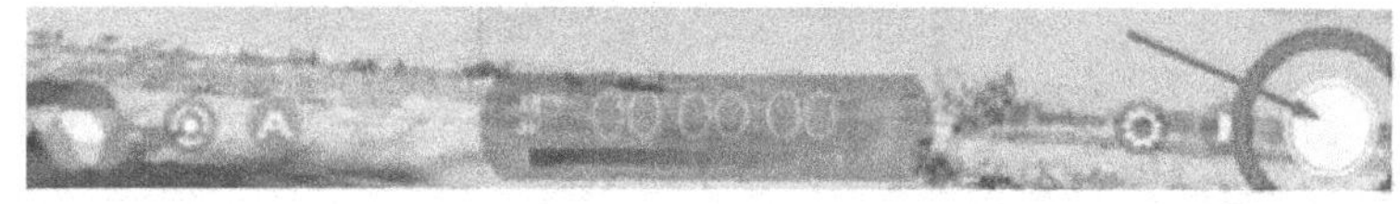

Click on the record button highlighted in red. Tap the same button highlighted in red to stop recording.

Playback and Clip menu

Open the FilMic library by clicking on the play button next to the record button. From the library, you can view all of your pre-recorded video. Tap on any of the clip to open it. You can edit the clip from the library. There are several clip editing tools in the FilMic pro; such as scissors tool, image adjustment tools etc.

Scissors tools

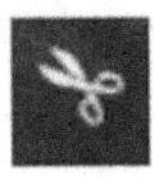

The scissors tool allows users to trim any clip of choice.

Image adjustment tools

This allows users to make adjustment to exposure, contrast, saturation and tint in the FilMic pro app.

About Author

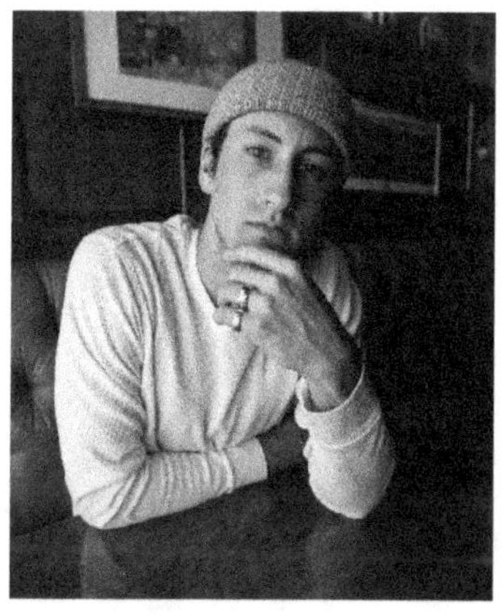

Donald Ray found his passion at the forefront of a new wave of filmmakers, harnessing his creative skills towards teaching others the basic skills of videography. He is an expert on making cinematic video and photography. He owns an online forum where he teaches beginners how to make videos and creating scripts.

Donald holds a Bachelor degree in information Electrical engineering from the University of Washington, USA. He is happily married with two kids.

www.ingramcontent.com/pod-product-compliance
Lightning Source LLC
Chambersburg PA
CBHW051435150726
48000CB00005B/2112